TIME EXPOSURE

TIME EXPOSURE

The
Personal Experience
of Time in Secular Societies

Richard K. Fenn

OXFORD
UNIVERSITY PRESS

2001

OXFORD

Oxford New York

Athens Auckland Bangkok Bogotá Bombay Buenos Aires
Calcutta Cape Town Dar es Salaam Delhi Florence Hong Kong
Istanbul Karachi Kuala Lumpur Madras Madrid Melbourne
Mexico City Nairobi Paris Shanghai Singapore Taipei Taipei Tokyo Toronto

and associated companies in
Berlin Ibadan

Copyright © 2001 by Richard K. Fenn

Published by Oxford University Press, Inc.,
198 Madison Avenue, New York, New York 10016

Oxford is a registered trademark of Oxford University Press

Library of Congress Cataloging-in-Publication Data
Fenn, Richard K.
Time exposure : a study of the personal experience of time in
secular societies / Richard Fenn.
p. cm.
Included bibliographical references and index.
ISBN 0-19-513953-4
1. Time—Religious aspects—Christianity—History of doctrines.
2. Time—Social aspects—History.
3. Secularization—History.   I. Title.
BT78 F36 2000
261—dc21   00-020716

1 3 5 7 9 8 6 4 2

Printed in the United States of America
on acid-free paper

FOR DAVID MARTIN

Acknowledgments

As the dedication of this book acknowledges, I owe to David Martin a debt of gratitude that this book itself cannot repay. David Martin has shown me what my eye would otherwise have missed along remote roads in the English countryside and in public squares. The markers of time and space have a code that David Martin has traced to Christianity itself. It is a code, I believe, that he has broken. More than his insight and his writing, it is his friendship that has been a source of grace. I may have been wiser as a result of his friendship, but I have been more appreciative of life itself. It is strange that I should dedicate a book such as this, in which I question the notion of providence, to someone whose friendship has been providential.

Among other friends and colleagues I want to be quick to mention James Moorhead, the historian of American Christianity at Princeton Theological Seminary. If anyone knows that public and private times no longer move to the same beat or rhythm, it is Jim Moorhead. Besides, like David Martin, he brings humor and grace to moments that would otherwise be too serious to be either good or true.

Cynthia Read at Oxford University Press has brought her own interest and enthusiasm to this publication. It is in its current shape largely because of her advice and patience. Every author should have such an editor at least once in his or her lifetime. I also want to thank Theo Calderara and Robin Miura, who made sure that my problems, from gaining publishers' permissions to finding the right words for an obscure thought, were solved easily and—on their part —gracefully. And every professor should have a research assistant like Marianne Delaporte, who for this work, and for two forthcoming volumes, has proved resourceful, encouraging, and effective in all her assistance.

I have two other debts that are more obscure but equally important. One is to psychoanalyst John Ordway who taught me as much as he could, under the circumstances, about the ways in which the unconscious plays games with time. The other is to my dear wife and friend, Cally, who has understood and lived with my obsessions with time for years on end without losing patience or affection.

Contents

TIME EXPOSURE

Introduction

The Meaning of Secularization

IT WOULD TAKE A FULL-LENGTH essay merely to review the literature on the topic of secularization; it is not only large and complex but controversial and of varied quality. The time has come for a thorough rethinking of the topic. In this book I am simply proposing that such a reconsideration focus merely on one aspect of secularization: the individual's experience of time. I will argue that secularization exposes the individual to the experience of the passage of time without the benefits of institutions that claim a certain transcendence over time itself. Whether it is in the experience or expression of grief and mourning or in the many contexts in which individuals are required to wait, individuals in secularized societies have less social protection from the burdens and force of time. Life increasingly becomes simply a matter of time.

The Church (not Christianity per se) was largely responsible for creating in the West a world in which organizations, institutions, and the state seemed to transcend the passage of time, whereas individuals became marginal, temporal, expendable. In the effort to administer a large and complex organization with claims to universality, the Church not only introduced high levels of rationality to systems of law and governance but focused on technical matters of procedure and precedent—highly pragmatic concerns in which the transcendental aim can easily be lost. In the past, sociologists have often referred to these instrumental concerns and activities as secular since they are means rather than ends, but this usage has also caused some confusion. That is because means may be intrinsic to ends, or they may become sacred in their own right, especially when they are highly ritualized. It is this rational, continuous administration of social life that gave the Church and the state the appearance of immunity to change, disruption, novelty, and chance. Thus, the so-called secular world of bureaucracies and the state appeared transcendent, whereas individuals per se were left to suffer the passage of time on their own. That world of transcendent administration laid claim to a providential or historical right to survey and dispose of human affairs. It is a world that has become itself visibly contingent: temporal and subject to both chance and change.

Christianity in general and the Church in particular are thus not the victims of this secularity; they have indeed slowly brought it over centuries of effort to get each generation to adopt Christianity as an act of faith rather than to rely on received tradition. Thus, the Church has endowed individuals with great spiritual responsibility and the right to think for themselves—rights and responsibilities that have led many an individual out from the shadow of the Church's teaching and authority. Even in societies and communities where Christianity has been well established, the central tendency of liberal Christianity, at least, has been to place individuals in situations in which they must rely on the spirit rather than on the law for guidance. In Christian discipleship the existential stakes are always high. One is left with full responsibility for choices that must be made without the guidance of rule or precedent.

In his work on Christianity and in Eastern Europe, David Martin (1990) has shown that dissenting Christians, Pentecostal and otherwise, habitually tend to create what he calls "open spaces." These are networks of mutual aid that enhance personal responsibility for breaking old forms of bondage to local authorities and personal addictions; they also create space for the future to open up through education, communication, and investment. Indeed, one central tendency of Christianity has been toward forging a society that is open to novelty and disruption, uncertainty and chance. Such a society requires a social character that is correspondingly open to high levels of ambiguity, existential tension, and the passage of time. In the hands of dissenting Christianity, at least, there is no narcissistic illusion that the larger society provides a spiritual home for the individual; just the contrary, in fact, is their central conviction.

It is no wonder, then, that some religious groups and movements seek to offer individuals moments of escape from the passage of time; promises of a millennial rapture offer the promise of transcendence at the expense of others for whom the day of judgment, unfortunately, has come. I will speak of these briefly later in the book. Even millennialists, however, find it necessary to make plans for the future, invest in their children's educations, and make communities worth living in for the next generation.

Beyond these pragmatic considerations, however, is the secularity deeply encoded in the core documents and traditions of Christianity itself. Western religion, I will argue, requires one to live by faith, and faith itself offers no providential shelter from the relentless passage of time and from death itself. Faith also requires one to live in this world with compassion and responsibility. For the Christian, the ordinary is never merely mundane.

That the process of secularization is rooted in Western religious traditions has long been argued. Christianity's demystification of the universe, its strong intentions for history, its tendency to systematize religious and secular beliefs and practices, its insistence on individual self-discipline, its appeal to an indigenous anticlericalism or laicism, and its intensification of individual responsibility for the use of time have all been conducive to a secular notion of nature and history.

Of course, Christians have been in little doubt that history tended toward divine judgment and a heavenly consummation; providence has figured largely in their historical reflections, if primarily in retrospect. Furthermore, when well established in a region, Christians have not been left to their own devices to find their way through the major crises in life or to grieve for the dead. Indeed, the Church's insistence on its own rites for these passages has often been rigorous and even imperial. In secularizing indigenous piety and bringing all devotion into systematic harmony with doctrine, the Church has sought to unite the private and the public in ways that would allow individuals the conviction that their pain registered in high places.

With secularization, however, the capacity of the Church to mobilize private devotion for public purposes and its capacity to define the nation's history have been greatly weakened.

That weakening, however, is not merely the result of alien forces that erode the Church's social foundations. It is due to central tendencies within Christianity itself. Christians' notion of a highly transcendent God left vast arrays of history and nature without visible signs of transcendence. The secular world became, by theological definition, the world that is subject to the passage of time and is thus forever passing away. In good conscience, then, the Church, as the successor to the Roman Empire, tended to destroy competition from other devotions and to discipline the plebeians. Christianity uprooted and destroyed indigenous piety when the bishop became the successor to the Roman governor or magistrate.

There were other reasons that the Church had a tendency to destroy or co-opt indigenous religion by bringing it within the precincts and control of the Christian clergy. In taking over the functions of administration, of managing conflict, and of providing a modicum of health, education, and welfare, the Church often found itself at odds with local customs and pieties. The indigenous and the local were thus seen as anomalies: outside the sweep of the Providence of God and destined to be discarded by sacred history. The Church's ideology thus allowed it to secularize local traditions by making them appear to be retrograde, outdated, superseded by the victory of Christ over all demigods, and thus inadequate to stand the test of time.

However, in this process the Church itself was changed into an institution that was subject to the world in which it lived, open to the passions and needs of the people, no matter how responsible it was to local aristocracies and officials. The Church, like Greek and Roman religion before it, became what Vico (1984:362) called "the sect of their times. . . . For the customs of the age are the school of princes . . . to use the term [*saeculum*, age] applied by Tacitus . . . to the decayed sect of his own times."

In this book I will argue that secularization has weakened—at times seemed to obliterate—the tension between this world and the next, between time and eternity. By the time of the Reformation, what Weber called the ascetic struggle between this-worldly and other-worldly allegiances still provided a peculiar dynamism to everyday life, to work and politics. However, with the secularization of time, this vertical tension, so to speak, became replaced by the horizontal. Individuals became obligated to show that they had redeemed their hours and days with useful activity as well as with devotions. The Protestant ethic marks just such a transition from an obsession with the past to obsessive preoccupation with the productive use of time. As Steve Bruce (1996:16) reminds us, "Each individual had to take a passionate interest in assessing his or her conduct. Many of the English Puritans kept detailed diaries in which they daily recorded evidences of their spiritual state." The transition was not from a cyclical view of time to a linear one. We can ignore the tendency of some, like Bruce (1996:16) himself, who continue to insist that an earlier agrarian world, based on the rotation of seasons, was giving way to a more industrial—and hence linear—time line. We know that even in the Middle Ages peasants had a quite realistic view of time as linear.[1] Rather, the transition was to a seriousness about the present and future that was quite as punctilious as the prior preoccupation with the past.

Some sociologists and anthropologists have tended in the past to regard certain societies as premodern. These lesser societies were therefore seen as being not only less complex than the social scientists' own societies but as therefore already outdated. It was just such a colonial strategy that marked the Church's response to the local pieties of Western Europe. Now, however, sociologists and anthropologists know that societies once seen as "traditional" as opposed to modern, or local instead of national or global, are also relatively complex and contemporaneous, with more possibilities and resources than had previously been imagined (Wallerstein 1996:83–84). "If social science is an exercise in the search for universal knowledge, then the 'other' cannot logically exist, for the 'other' is part of 'us'—the us that is studied, the us that is engaged in studying" (Wallerstein 1996:57). This is not a sentiment that would have graced official theological reflection on the pagan world at any stage in Church history—and certainly not in the formative centuries when the Church was bent on superseding all local forms of government, authority, and piety. The secular world was the "other": the world without hope of transcending time, destined to pass away to extinction, and beyond the pale of grace and providence.

Despite its strong ideological connotations, I am retrieving the notion of the secular to represent the experience of being temporal. That experience may range from the awareness of mere transience to sheer terror at the prospect of annihilation. Some people, of course, are merely aware of the shortness of life and appear to accept it, while others face the prospect of death with acute dread. Events may make a drastic change in one's life or the life of one's community or nation; conversely, life may go on without apparent interruption from one period or generation to the next. Thus, the experience of time may be sudden and disruptive or continuous and merely corrosive. Some individuals may be aware of the slow decline of their own abilities and energy, just as communities or nations experience themselves as developing, stagnant, or in decline. Others, both individuals and peoples, may experience time most acutely as disruptive events. I do not propose here to develop an entire typology of the experience of temporality; that would be far beyond the scope of this book. It is the sheer subjection to the passage of time, in whatever form, that defines the experience of secularity.

Moreover, as I am using the term, secularity also carries with it the notion of being marginal to the institutions and social systems that lay a claim to transcending the passage of time. The Church created the secular world by turning it into the "other": the very opposite of the Church that claimed to have a purchase on eternity. But the Church is not the only institution that claims this sort of transcendence and in so doing creates a secular world on its margins. The state, the family, those who defend certain values or ways of life are all prone to an ideological depiction of secularity as that which cannot stand the test of time and is therefore bound to pass away. It is no wonder, then, that those who have been thus secularized return the ideological insult by claiming that it is they and their own ways of life that will transcend the time and that the larger society is the one destined for extinction, millennialists being an obvious case in point.

Disease and accident, social change and conflict, the movement of people and ideas can all turn life into a confusing welter of threat and possibility. It is just these "chaotic realities" that expose the individual to the passage and force of time and once made the world of bureaucrats and priests seem relatively immune to time itself. Now, however, even the world of large-scale social systems is complex and changing, filled with chance and uncertainty. The institutions that claimed to have a purchase on providence and the right to oversee social life have become visibly subject to the passage of time. The Church that once found local pieties to be anomalous has joined the ranks of the expendable.

It is not only the Church and its ideology that have secularized "the world." Religious ecstasy tends to make the world itself seem suspect and counterfeit, flimsy and temporal. The ecstatic becomes marginal to the social order and sees it as having relatively little to do with the individual's own psyche and character, values and beliefs. Conversely, those on the margins of the social order may develop their own forms of piety to offset the religious claims of the political and cultural center:

> [T]he Mahayana Buddhist application of the concept of "maya" to the state, the powerful, and the ruling clans disproves the omnipresence of the logic of power, predominant among the monotheist discourses. The Daoist concept of the legitimate "path" (*dao*) conceives legitimacy as an existential association with the chaotic realities beyond the bureaucratic legitimacy of Confucianism (Wallerstein 1996: 56–57).

Certainly we are used to thinking of secularity as a heroic stance against spiritual predators who intrude on the privacy of the soul or co-opt the anxious mind with authoritative reassurance. Conversely, many in the churches still imagine the secular world to be something over and against the Church: an opposing source of (false) meaning that impedes the work of the Church and allows conscience to be deluded and undeveloped. This reactionary attack on the secular world will no doubt continue, regardless of the social changes that I wish to discuss in this book, if only because the Church needs to feel itself in agonistic struggle with a "world" that has needs that the Church alone can fill and that embodies the sort of darkness that only the Church's light can dispel.

In the formative years of the Church during the fourth and fifth centuries, Christian beliefs and rites, the Church's sense of mission, and its powerful administrative apparatus all were given a shape that has persisted over nearly fifteen centuries. The Church became the heir apparent to Roman civilization and power. Even before Constantine gave the Church legitimacy and priority, elites had found their way into the Church, and the Church's leadership was increasingly competent to adjudicate civil conflicts, keep peasants in order, and administer the health, education, and welfare of the people in their jurisdiction (Fletcher 1997:37–38).

When a single institution has the oversight of so many aspects of social life, a doctrine of providence will make unique and compelling sense. Very little that occurred, whether by way of natural disaster or chronic social conflict, occurred outside the scope of the Church's overseeing eye; the episcopate—as the name implies—was charged with oversight and carried it out with rigor and some success. By the fifth century, bishops were in control not only of the sinner and the heretic but also of the powerful civic and military offices. A bishop of Auxerre, one Germanus, not only supervised heresy and taxation; he also mounted military expeditions (Fletcher 1997:50). Not only did vocations to the priesthood seem to increase rapidly in the fourth century and after, as the Church became a pathway to jobs and pensions, but even the peasantry found it in their interest to seek salvation within the Church. The Church, in a sense, did provide for the material as well as spiritual well-being of many of its adherents.

Certainly the Church held Christian landlords responsible for the civility and compliance of their tenants. Fletcher (1997:51) notes that "[i]f official Christianity was, increasingly with the passing years, what gave cohesion and identity to a community there was some inducement to throw in your lot with it. Rural conversion, like many other varieties of conversion to Christianity (or other faiths), partook of something of the nature of joining a club." Another way to put this is that religion was not differentiated from the other aspects of social life. It is not simply that the Church was at the service of military and civic authority, whereas previously it had been at their mercy. It is that the Church itself embodied aspects of civic and military authority just as had the Roman institutions that had once been the Church's enemy. Thus Fletcher (1997:118, 122) points out that the

Church commended the faith to various barbarian warlords as being essential for victory in battle, and the Church developed codes of law that embodied a mixture of Roman jurisprudence and the custom of the people. The Church was a providential institution in providing a framework for individual will and conflicting interests to be worked out.

Under these conditions, I would argue, Fletcher's analogy between conversion and joining a club is beside the point. Whereas clubs are voluntary organizations, there was often an element of implied coercion in conversions, especially when Roman bishops brought to bear their influence on an aspiring Gothic warlord, or Christian landlords impressed their wishes upon the peasantry. Furthermore, individuals who join clubs are—within the terms of Fletcher's analogy—modern souls, surrounded by a culture that respects individuality and fosters a high degree of self-determination. The individuals of whom Fletcher writes, landholding nobles, Gothic warlords, peasants under overwhelming obligations to their lords and with few alternatives to obedience, were enmeshed in webs of social affiliation that made it difficult for them to act alone. Hence, even warlords took their time before committing themselves (and their families, their fellow lords, and perhaps their peasants) to the new faith, and they needed to be assured of the advantages of Roman administration and of the favor of the Christian god in battle. There was a lot more at stake than club membership; all their social, emotional, political, economic, and religious eggs were in one basket or another. Contrast the multiple sorts of membership and affiliation that are open to individuals in complex, modern societies. Relatively few people have all their social and emotional eggs in one institutional or communal basket.

Now believers may believe without going to church, and churchgoers may or may not become members of religious institutions, let alone adhere to the official confession or creed of their Church. There is a rough-and-ready spiritual egalitarianism at work that allows one to say without diffidence or apology that one's own version of the faith is as valid as anyone's else, including the clergy's more highly rationalized and official account of the tradition. The individual who used to be able to say, without fear of social embarrassment, "I may not know much about art but I know what I like," can now say that also about religion. Steve Bruce (1996:5) states it simply enough: "Individualism has encroached on the definition of reality.... We claim not only the right to do what is right in our own eyes but to assert that the world is as we variously see it.... [Religion has evolved into] a cosmic consciousness which can be claimed as the underlying reality beneath whatever deviant and divergent visions one may have." Not merely an offshoot of the Enlightenment, individualism was the core principle of the Reformation, with each person required to take responsibility for his or her own standing in the eyes of God. One had to prepare for one's own awful encounter with the Deity unaided except by faith and the sacrifice of the Son of God for one's sins. Gone was the mediation, so to speak, of the Church's sacramental system.

The individual now has access to divine grace without the benefit or hindrance of the clergy; one is responsible for one's own spiritual fate. If the cathedrals—and the Church generally—have come to seem more like empty institutional shells than sanctuaries both from earthly and divine punishment, it is because the individual has emerged from the protection—and the shadow—of the church into the full current of time. If, as Bruce (1996:22, 43) puts it, the Reformation "removed the institution of the Church as a source of authority between God and man," individuals must now come to their own terms with the Bible, the Church, and their own vocation: "[O]ne of the great innovations of the Protestant Reformation was the idea that we are all able to discern God's will for ourselves. We do not need a professional cadre of priests to do that for us."

While it is often the Church that decries modern individualism, it was the Church that created it by making the individual responsible for working out his or her own salvation without drawing on a treasury of spiritual merit stored up in the institution of the Church itself. The same drive toward freeing the individual from background institutions has produced an egalitarian impulse that levels a number of moral and aesthetic distinctions that used to accompany social class. Few now would argue that the lower orders are morally deficient or that the well-to-do have an aesthetic out of the reach of the ordinary citizen. Scandal, the public exposure of the elite through the media, and the general accessibility of fine art in public museums and on television have collapsed these background distinctions into a perennial foreground.[2] Individuals now must stand on their own ground. No wonder that so many adopt the camouflage of public taste and public opinion.

The notion of a Protestant ethic that embodies an acute sense of responsibility for the affairs of this world rested, as Weber noted, on an asceticism that placed this world in chronic tension with the world beyond. Eliminate that tension, and the ascetic struggle becomes more visibly a matter of internal division within the psyche, a division amenable to this-worldly cure.

Secularization takes the mystery out of time. In the first chapter I will suggest that attempts to mystify the passage of time are inherently ideological, in the sense that they give one society or way of life an apparent advantage over others that are seen as outmoded or underdeveloped. True secularity, I will argue, accepts that societies are inherently self-made and that they serve no providential purpose. True secularity also accepts a psychological divorce, as it were, between the individual and the larger society. The terms of the divorce stipulate that the individual will not be able to take narcissistic satisfaction from collective illusions about the importance of the larger society; one implication of this settlement is that the larger society will have more difficulty in placing sacrificial demands on the individual.

In the second chapter I expand on this theme by drawing particularly on the work of T. S. Eliot to describe the sense of the temporal as what is lasting in secular societies. Private grief is no longer articulated in public mourning, and memory becomes more fluid and personal rather than enshrined in public monuments.

In the third chapter I continue to explore the ways that institutions continue to construe time and to show how these depart from the ways in which individuals experience time. This disjunction is rooted in aspects of the Christian tradition that free the individual from the mediation of religious institutions like the Church that seek to relate the vicissitudes of everyday life to a providential sphere. Secularity is not the undoing of the Christian tradition, then, so much as its final fruit.

Of course, that tradition is not seamless with regard to its understanding of time; instead, it is filled with internal contradictions, and these, too, have had their long-term social consequences. I explore these contradictions in more detail in chapters four and five, which are devoted to the topic of waiting. There I will point out that ritual once was able to intensify and complete the process of waiting within definite time limits. In more ritualized and complex societies, however, waiting becomes a way of life that marginalizes individuals and heightens their awareness that the social order is largely self-made rather than providential. Under these conditions individuals are understandably inventive and even idiosyncratic in managing their anxieties about time and mortality.

In the sixth chapter I will argue that the "temporal" is losing its connotations of being in tension with the eternal; secularity understands the temporal to be primarily—and merely—a matter of time. Thus secularization represents the progressive loss of collective illusions, forms of self-deception, and culturally supported lies. Communal fantasies once allowed the social order to seem timeless—at least when compared with the secular, that is, temporal, life of the (mere) individual. Now these illusions have lost their capacity to give the individual a temporal home that foreshadows the eternal. One is left without the narcissistic satisfaction of knowing that one's earthly sacrifices really matter. One is also left without the tension between this world and the next.

ONE

Time Will Tell
The Meaning Of Secularity

FOR THE MYSTIC, AS FOR THE PRIMITIVE, the world is only partly disenchanted. There is always a hint of a time before time: the primordial period that underlies all later calculations and passages. The process of enchantment thus begins when one takes a particular experience out of the flux of everyday life in order to give it sacred meaning. Perhaps it was a moment in which insight dawned or a discovery was made; any experience of peculiar and lasting intensity can become momentous.

To enshrine time in this way is an antidote, based on magical thinking, to the prospect of losing time once and for all. That is why some dates may "live in infamy" while others have a happier place in the canon of memory, but they all succeed in making an event of the past into a continuing and present reality: a time long gone that one nonetheless experiences in the present. Many individuals remember not only the date on which John Kennedy was shot, but also what they were doing on that day and where they were doing it. Others remember with equal clarity other dates: Pearl Harbor and D-Day or the day that Martin Luther King was assassinated. These dates, however, are not simply tokens or reminders of events in the past. Marked with ceremony and reenactment, we speak of them in a special voice. No longer the real thing, nonetheless the original day is reenacted in the present as though time itself were not lost or entirely irreversible. Hence, the periodic anxiety in England, for instance, over anniversaries of the Easter rising, when the Irish declared their independence of British rule. It is an anxiety that may still give rise to stringent security measures. In any event, the refusal to allow the date to be eclipsed by the passage of time and the tendency to enshrine it in sacred memory is precisely what I mean by the opposite of secularity. It constitutes a rebellion against the passage of time.

Secularity is at best an acquired taste. I take up a discussion of secularity in this book simply because secularity is uniquely suited to the uncertainties of modern social life. This is not to say that a secular social character will be easy to come by as a natural form of adaptation to complexity. On the contrary, the rebellion against time is more widespread than the secular submission to the passage of time. It is far too difficult to "wait without thought" or to "wait without hope," far too difficult to "go through the way in which you are not,'" as Eliot (1943:00) put it. There is a longing, as widespread as it is deeply entrenched in the psyche, for access to primordial time.

Thus, it is easy to enshrine certain moments, especially when they are accompanied with affections that die hard. Such experiences may go into a psychic underground where feelings are not really dated. There they have a life of their own and add a dimension of seriousness to other moments and experiences that might otherwise be wholly unrelated. It is the return of this "undated" emotion and fantasy that underlies anticipatory grief and the more general feeling that something momentous may be about to happen. Memory and recollection may then rekindle an old affection, or words spoken in anger may come back to haunt the speaker. Lovers remember the moment when they first laid eyes upon each other.

Once enshrined, these past events and experiences seem contemporary with current experience. Such is often the case with events that are shocking and traumatic: a sudden death, the outburst of violence, a volcanic eruption or a sudden flood, for example; they become "like yesterday." These may be times when an insight dawned or a revelation was given, a decision was made or an action undertaken, a king died, a portent appeared or an angel passed overhead. Those who were not even present at such a time may feel as if they, too, are living in a world in which that past event is an important part of their own experience. If, for instance, the collective repertoire of events includes a flood, a revelation, or the death of a king, these events may be embodied in a round of rituals and in a sacred calendar. The momentous is then reenacted regularly in a particular cycle of events, the full meaning and prescriptions of which are known, perhaps, only to a relative few who are entrusted with sacred knowledge. Under these official auspices, time may become divided into the full and the empty, the sacred and the profane, the eventful and the merely busy or tedious. Almanacs and horoscopes are further aids in divining the times by creating segments that are auspicious for certain activities and dangerous for others. To enter fully into time requires a secular discipline that frees one from these earlier loves and hurts, dreams and attachments.

Old fears and trauma seem to live in a time of their own that is peculiarly resilient. At various times in the years in which I have been working on this book, it has seemed as if there might soon be another war in the Middle East. There have been times of wondering what will happen to the price of oil; the price of oil fluctuates according to the perception that war may or may not be inevitable. There have also been times of tentative and anticipatory grief. The prospect of more deaths and body bags has sometimes been in the offing. There has been the prospect of a war that might be as unnecessary as it would be destructive; there has also been the prospect of unlimited possibilities for terror and the mass destruction of human life both at home and abroad. Waiting, and with it an unrelieved exposure to the passage of time, is of the essence of a secular world.

Individuals who live in secular societies therefore have no illusion that their own societies represent the people's values and convictions, their commitments and ideals. Politics becomes a contingency game because any decision that is taken might not have been taken; no outcome is necessary or foreordained or inevitable, just as no one had to decide to test or drop the first atomic bomb. No one knows the full range of possibilities that currently exists, just as no one knew ahead of time whether the fission released from the first atomic bomb test would get out of control and produce a global meltdown. As Niklas Luhmann (1995:106) puts it, the "concept of contingency . . . results from excluding necessity and impossibility." That leaves open an indefinite prospect of time in which it is necessary, above all, to wait.

There is an understandable terror that comes from knowing that one is operating in a field of possibilities that is open; no one knows what the sum of these possibilities may be, let alone which of them might be chosen by the other players of the game. When the players are a government and a loose organization of terrorist networks with dispersed training sites and transnational loyalties, the uncertainty increases to the limits of human toleration. There is no final authority that can know and judge the decisions of the players, and there is no limit to the possible administration of terror. That is why Luhmann (1995:105) speaks of the field as being "empty, closed, indeterminable self-reference."

Therefore, to imagine a secular society, think of a pair of individuals who have no information about each other at all; each is totally in the dark, so to speak, about the other's intentions and feelings, wishes and aspirations. Calling them alter and ego, Luhmann (1995: 104–5) describes them as building a social system out of nothing:

> At first, alter tentatively determines his behavior in a situation that is still unclear. He begins with a friendly glance, a gesture, a gift—and waits to see whether and how ego receives the proposed definition of the situation. In light of this beginning, every subsequent step is an action with a contingency-reducing, determining effect—be it positive or negative.... We can connect this with the "order from noise principle" of general systems theory. No preordained value consensus is needed; the problem of double contingency (i.e., empty, closed, indeterminable self-reference) draws in chance straightaway, creates sensitivity to chance, and when no value consensus exists, one can thereby invent it. The system emerges etsi non daretur Deus [even if God does not exist]. (emphasis added)

Note that the system is self-referential. It does not represent the full range of possibilities that their interaction opens up. There is no outside authority that can set limits on what they can do, no definitions that can limit what they may mean. Thus, the system between them takes on a life of its own; it becomes—like the computer, Hal, in Stanley Kubrick's space film, *2001*—self-made and self-referential.

Imagine, for the moment, that the two players are Iraq and the United States. Madeleine Albright is trying to send a message to Saddam Hussein by speaking into the cameras of CNN, the news network that presented the Gulf War to international viewers and that is watched carefully from the highest offices in Baghdad. She is like the "alter" whom Luhmann (1995:104) mentioned, who "begins with a friendly glance, a gesture, a gift—" not knowing how Saddam ("ego") will act. The "world" consists of the empty space between these two players in which the expectations and actions of the one may have little, if any, capacity to constrain the other. Relying on past behavior as a guide to the present may be fatally misleading since neither side is constrained by precedent. Of course, Albright might hope that a Russian ambassador or a moderate cabinet member in the Iraqi government might help to determine Hussein's behavior, but Albright has no way of knowing what sort of pressure might be applied or what sort of response Hussein might make. He is capable of killing any messenger and of responding with unrestrained and relentless brutality and/or with canny and calculated self-interest.

Here we have what Luhmann (1995:103ff.) calls "the problematic of double contingency," and he compares it to two black boxes talking to each other. By these boxes I take Luhmann to refer to two computers; his images are cybernetic, and they make sense if one imagines that a secular social system is like the Internet: a series of possible relationships, all of which are contingent on the decisions, choices, principles of selection, and responses of people who are opaque to one another. It is like being alone in the dark with a stranger. Thus, a secular society can make one very anxious indeed. However, in the case of Albright and Hussein, the problem of double contingency becomes "acute," as Luhmann (1995:106) puts it: "an endlessly open possibility of meaning determination that eludes access from the outside."

Of course, "modern" societies are not the first to provide this indeterminate set of possibilities in which it is necessary to "wait and see" because "time will tell." First-century Israel was not one but several social systems, each interpenetrating the others: the Roman, the Hellenistic, the Jewish, each with its own internal divisions and complexity. If in Jesus Christ there were neither Jew nor Greek, it is clear that for the Jew to treat the other as a Greek, and the other to treat the Jew as a Jew, would have entailed missing the range of possibility that had been discovered in the early Christian communities. It was the open spaces, as it were, that were beckoning the Christian: possibilities of a new relationship in which it was yet to be seen what people would or could become. If in Jesus Christ there were neither male nor female, then the future of gender relationships would remain to be seen; at any given time a fixed sense of what it means— socially speaking—to be a man or woman would be to miss the Christian point. One has to wait and see what one is to become—in the course of being with others. In the meantime, however, one is anything but passive, but is actively sending out signals to other "black boxes" in the hope of receiving a signal in return that will help to define the message that one has just sent.

When a secular social system emerges, therefore, it is without the necessity or possibility of God. There is no possibility of appealing to an outside and higher authority to legitimate one decision or another. All choices are equally possible; indeed, as Dostoyevsky put it, if God is dead everything is possible, and nothing is "given" or necessary. It is just such an existentialist's notion of society that Luhmann is placing at the center of his theory.

A secular society, then, has two characteristics. The first is that no one can stand apart from it and claim to view the society as a whole from some transcendent vantage point. There is no sacred history that can be invoked, no ideological notion of the nation's place in history, that can be used to account for the strengths and failings of the society as a whole. Instead, the society clearly generates its own beliefs and standards, and these are marked with the stamp of time. Any values, any institutions, any laws and codes of conduct are thus clearly the work of the society itself and not the residues of some transcendent legacy. They are also clearly dated: provisional, temporary, and intended to be changed over time. I will call this the loss of the providential viewpoint whether or not the providence in question was thought to be divine or the logic of some immanent historical process.

The second characteristic, I will argue, is that the society itself no longer can claim to represent values that represent and yet transcend the individual. That means that the larger society no longer stands for the enduring aspects of the self. It also means that individuals can no longer see a dignified or even exalted representation of themselves in the values and beliefs, the institutions and the codes of the larger society. As a result, individuals are left to their own devices to find a way of transcending the passage of time. I will call this the loss of the narcissistic viewpoint; societies no longer serve the purpose of a mirror for the self.

The exposure to a nonprovidential world in which a society no longer gives the individual narcissistic guarantees and satisfactions immerses the individual in the passage of time. Individuals cannot step out of their societies and view them from above, as it were. Instead, individuals correctly see their own societies as provisional and pragmatic collections of rules and resources organized to suit the needs of some more than others. In the jargon of the social sciences, societies are self-organizing and self-referential. Similarly, the exposure to such a social system leaves the individual without any societal mirror in which to see the self magnified to collective proportions. Individuals will have to look somewhere besides major institutions and creeds for a symbol or statement of who they are, what they are about, and why they should be remembered.

These two changes, taken together, account for much of the fatigue of religious traditions, at least in the Christianized West. Consider in particular the biblical view of history as unfolding the wisdom and providence of God. The Bible itself speaks of the temporal from the vantage point of a God whose purposes are at work in the most hopeless and damaging of circumstances. People may have "meant it for evil, but God meant it for good"; that motif from the Joseph story runs throughout both the Old Testament and the New: God so gave His only Son . . ." The biblical view regards even the most tragic and painful of events in everyday life as part of the divine plan. No matter whether it was incursions from outside—such as from Persia or Rome—or atrocities from within, every new event is coded "as an ingredient of the divine plan . . . the various components all belong to one concept of universal history and its interpretation" (Auerbach 1953:17). Even though the early Christian community, under Paul, revised its understanding of Israel and its history, the framework was not broken but simply expanded to include the Christians themselves as the new—and the true—Israel. The divine will has been at work again, taking the events that are of no account in this world and making them the pivotal moment of history itself. Thus, the horrors of the period prior to the coming of Christ can themselves be seen as part of a divine plan; earlier sacrifices and heroism were performed by people whose significance is anything but concrete and particular, and whose lives are worthwhile only because they prefigure the coming of Christ himself.

To see the past as prefiguring the present turns the present into the completion of what had hitherto only been foreshadowed. This providential viewpoint combines the existential with the historical without critical self-reflection. The result is patently ideological: a failure to see that societies are self-referential and self-organizing rather than the result of a prior and superior will at work in the struggles of one society or another. One can see other societies as being outmoded or less "developed." The colonized represent the past of the colonial regime, which is then entitled to complete the work of development by correcting the deficiencies of the indigenous society: that is the providential view.

It is the same stance taken by the expanding Western Church toward local communities and their pagan devotions. We should therefore not be surprised to find that under ecclesiastical and aristocratic auspices even the popular poetry of the early Middle Ages took on the view "from above," a distance from the ordinary, the immediate, concrete, particular, and practical matters of everyday life that had characterized Greco-Roman epic poetry a millennium earlier. It is a style in which "[c]lass limitation, idealization, simplification, and the shimmering veil of legend prevail" (Auerbach 1953:121).

This development does discount the experience of ordinary people, ignore the mundane, and thus provide a certain immunity from the passage of time; it is a move away from secularity, even though, as Auerbach (1953:121) insists, the epic poetry was enormously popular "among the lower classes." The religious movement that had plunged its followers into the temporal was now achieving a certain distance from the everyday in the interest of social order and control. It was also increasingly bent on imposing its own meaning and logic on the course of history. Thus, the need to see that societies reflect the mind and the will of God allowed the Church also to sustain a narcissistic viewpoint about its own society—for instance, to see it as guaranteeing the believer's own place in history and thus to see other classes, communities, or peoples as being on the losing side of time.

The New Testament does make a concession, then, to the flow of time, but it is only a partial one. On the terms provided by the New Testament, the Christian is to read the Old as a succession of events that are related to each other through a divine plan. To see that relationship requires an act of faith, and so the Bible reveals its inner connections only to those with the necessary spiritual penetration. One can therefore understand David, for instance, or Joseph, only if one sees them as forerunners of Jesus, and one can understand Jesus only if one sees him as completing and correcting what came earlier in Joseph or David. As Auerbach (1953:73) puts it, "In practice we almost always find an interpretation of the Old Testament, whose episodes are interpreted as figures or phenomenal prophecies of the events of the New Testament." From the viewpoint of the writers of the New Testament, the prior history of the people of God was not only providential; it also referred to their own later advent. This narcissistic viewpoint allowed them to regard the history of an entire people as referring to their own eventual arrival on the historical stage. The Christian community could then regard the "old" Israel as having served its historical purpose; eventually it could be superseded by the later, Christian community.

To grasp the secular, then, is to understand that no people—and no moment in time—is given a historical preference or temporal privilege. For instance, consider Auerbach's discussion of a medieval romance, the *Chanson de Roland*. Auerbach (1953:96–142) finds a critical moment described in detail in a series of verses. The verses often begin the account all over again, even from the beginning, but in each verse a new meaning is brought out, a new layer of understanding, a new exposure of what lies below the surface of the words themselves. It is as if one has to take several exposures of the same moment to understand what is really happening. No particular account, no single verse, can claim priority over the other; no single viewpoint is privileged. Very much as a psychoanalyst would disinter layers of meaning, emotion, memory, and fantasy, the poet tells the story over and over again: "Time and again there is a new start; every resumption is complete in itself and independent; the next is simply juxtaposed to it, and the relation between the two is often left hanging" (Auerbach 1953:105).

One could say very much the same thing about the Synoptic Gospels, in which each new episode is connected with the previous one only by being placed next to it or by a thin editorial thread ("at that time," "in those parts") or with a connecting word like "then." It is not that the coherent story is missing or forgotten but simply that those involved in them do not have an inkling of the larger picture or the divine plan. As Bultmann put it in his commentary on the Gospel of John, the point is that any moment might—or might not—be sacred; to be secular is to know that one's entire life may—or may not—be defined by a particular moment. The moment may or may not be self-revelatory, may or may not provide a mirror of the outline and dimensions of one's own existence. In any event, there is no providential viewpoint from which to tell the story.

In suggesting that Christian providential notions no longer fit "modern" societies that are clearly self-made and self-justifying, it is necessary for me to be on guard against an implicitly providential viewpoint of my own. For instance, I might seem to be relegating biblical societies to a time when the world was enchanted with unseen forces, when spirits and demons invaded one's psychological premises, and when social life seemed particularly resistant to human efforts at knowledge and control. Certainly anthropologists have been particularly critical of their own tendencies to put social and psychological distance between themselves and the "primitives" with whom they have been conversing. The distance is often professionally required, of course, because the dialogue with the "primitive" later has to be translated and commented upon in a text meant for the consumption of academic peers and superiors. With that distancing comes a change of meaning disguised by the continued use of the present tense. Johannes Fabian (1983) points out that the so-called ethnographic present is therefore deceptive. In fact, the anthropologist relegates the "other" to the abstracted time of certain diagnostic categories or to the past, as if there were a natural history of social and psychological development over various stages that culminates in the time of the observer.

The anthropological use of the past not only provides the researcher with the appearance of psychological and social distance; it also places the anthropologist among the ranks of various colonial oppressors. Fabian (1983:63) is quite clear on this point: "Aside from the evolutionist figure of the savage there has been no conception more obviously implicated in political and cultural oppression than that of the childlike native. Moreover, what could be clearer evidence of temporal distancing than placing the Now of the primitive in the Then of the Western adult?" It is now the primitive who represents what the modern soul has overcome and transcended: a mess of magical thinking, for instance, or infantile illusions about one's place in the world. Because "primitives" therefore display an inability to draw a line between the self and the "other" or between the human and the natural, they are also thought to be unusually open to suggestion. Thus, the primitive self is easily displaced or captivated by powerful others and can be led into acts of self-mortification and self-sacrifice. Who among Westerners is like them, unless it be those who—being somewhat underdeveloped in their own psyches—are likely to be swayed by mass appeals from charismatic leaders like Adolf Hitler or James Jones? The primitive is still alive in the West, one might admit, but only in the category of "deviant" or "collective" behavior. At the very least, the academic might regard the fundamentalist as one who is unable to cope with the ambiguity and the complexity of the mature Westerner.

It is understandable that social scientists would be as likely as anyone else to feel that they, too, are running out of time in a world that is not providential and does not offer them the narcissistic satisfaction of reflecting their own values and commitments. It is an axiom of social science that individuals collectively produce their own social worlds and then live in them as if these worlds were given rather than made. If this childlike stance vis-à-vis their own productions no longer characterizes "modernity," it still can be found among many whose faith is primitive and who unwittingly engage in rituals that subordinate them to their own creations. As Fabian (1983:63) puts it: "[T]alk about the childlike nature of the primitive has never been just a neutral classificatory act, but a powerful rhetorical figure and motive, informing colonial practice in every aspect from religious indoctrination to labor laws and the granting of basic political rights." Children, furthermore, are not producers; whereas adults do produce, children consume and need protection from the rigors of adult responsibility. Thus, the analogy with children in discourse about the "primitive" places them in a past in which culture is "given" rather than produced. These imaginary others merely make choices in a world of less complexity and ambiguity than the presumably more modern and adult world of anthropologists. Conversely, it is the complexity of the anthropologists' world that enables them to classify the behavior of the "primitive" into one category or another. After all, it takes a principle of selection developed in complex societies to understand the relative degrees of lesser complexity in the less developed world to be studied.

Invidiously to compare the "primitive" with the moderns, who, like the social scientists, know that their social worlds are self-referential and self-producing may afford a few narcissistic satisfactions. This is precisely Fabian's (1983:65) point: "The key to understanding this view of empirical objectivity is its glorification of distance based on the denial of conditions of shared Time."

More than the anthropologist's self-referential categories come into play: potentially the full range of human longing, self-deception, and the exploitation of others for the enhancement of the self. It is the same for lovers or psychoanalysts or bureaucrats; only the varying conditions set limits on the extent to which power and imagination come into play. Psychoanalysts are in fact trained to know that both parties are engaged in such a self-referential production; thus, they have safeguards against any tendency to underestimate the resourcefulness, creativity, and maturity of their patients. The safeguards are there for a reason: the tendency to deny the involvement of both parties in sharing and producing the present in which they live is endemic not only to the analytic situation but to human encounters.

When analysis works, of course, both parties are deeply engaged in the mutual experience of each other's imagination and subjectivity. That is what Fabian means by the coeval; it is a shared time in which each person is exposed to the full range of the other's experience. It is necessary to be haunted, so to speak, by another's ghosts if one is to be able to live in the same world with the other—necessary, if one is simply to be able to understand.

To summarize: The Christian notion that the rest of the world is a mere "preparation for the Gospel" is not merely analogous to the contemporary notion that others are in a premodern or preindustrial world, while we are truly modern or even postmodern. In fact, Fabian is quite clear that the notion of a sacred history, in which the past is a prologue to the Christian present, was the source of secular views of history as evolutionary or developmental. Others (e.g., those in less "developed" societies) are thus reduced to living in a world that is at some steps removed from the present, even when they are our contemporaries, just as others who are our contemporaries are sometimes still reduced to living in a world that is pre-Christian. As Fabian (1983:35) puts it, it is terribly difficult for "the West" to admit that "the Rest" are the contemporaries and thus the peers of the West, except for some differences in the technology and the capacity for "economic exploitation."

The "modern" experience of time thus includes elements that are often regarded as more "traditional" or more "primitive." By "modern" I simply mean the employment of an abstract, uniform, and continuous notion of time, typified by clocks and Newtonian physics, an achievement, we now realize, that may have taken centuries to acquire but that children learn prior to adolescence (Friedman 1990:100). On the other hand, what Friedman (1990:109) calls our "psychological time" is difficult to distinguish from the temporal "experience of people in traditional cultures." For instance, Westerners are very much like members of more traditional societies in using particular, concrete events or experiences to date the past, rather than something more abstract.

It is difficult to separate the so-called modern world, with its allegedly linear and abstract notions of time, from the world still enmeshed in allegedly circular, recurrent, and concrete conceptions of time. Barbara Adam, an English sociologist who writes about "the analysis of time," argues, in fact, that the everyday life of Westerners is as permeated by the past and the future as that of other cultures. Westerners' sense of time, she argues, is quite filled with the eventful and cyclic, and the times in which one lives are both multiple and plastic.

In emphasizing that the rest of the world is contemporary with the West, we are discarding both the providential and the narcissistic viewpoints. That is, the West has no privileged position in time vis-à-vis the rest of the world: not as the culmination or end-in-view of some process of development; not as the avant-garde of social change that makes other societies outmoded or retrograde. The nation as a whole is neither the wave of the future nor the fulfillment of the past but a social system that generates itself and creates its own complexity in response to an increasingly uncertain and ambiguous environment. The loss of the providential viewpoint does indeed make the West contemporaneous with every other society, equally subject to the contingencies of the moment and to the passage of time.

This is not to say that the peoples of modern nations have lost any convictions that could be traced to a biblical or classical civilization. There is continuity at the level of the civilization, which is to say that some beliefs and values die hard when they are deeply entrenched in schools and families, the codes of neighborliness and civility, and the sense of what it means to be a responsible person over time. While governments may continue to evoke such rhetoric, however, it becomes increasingly clear to the so-called average citizen that managing the system takes precedence over various forms of decency.

The increasing tolerance of the American public for officials who are effective managers of the economy and are morally bankrupt is a case in point; the widespread European amusement or disbelief at American puritanism in such matters is another. It may well be that what died in the protests of the 1960s and in the assassinations of major public figures like the Kennedy brothers and Martin Luther King was the belief and the hope that the state and public officials would provide a satisfactory reflection of—and on—the individual.

It is nonetheless difficult to endure a historical prospect that does not predict or enshrine the nation and its institutions, just as a nation that no longer represents the beliefs and values of its citizens inflicts narcissistic wounds that some, at least, will find bearable but others will be unable to tolerate for long. It is difficult to know that one is running out of time—even more difficult to know that so is one's community and nation. A purely temporal prospect erodes the nation's place in history and the individual's place in the larger society. In *The Persistence of Purgatory* (1992) I mentioned Dickens's account of his travels to America. In that account he recalls standing on the edge of the Great Plains west of St. Louis. The prospect was interminable. The horizon, as it were, kept receding before him. In the foreground there were patches of bare earth and the remains of a convent that had been burned to the ground. Earlier he had commented on the "eternal foreground" that had chilled his spirit as he sailed toward St. Louis along the banks of the Ohio River. It is this open-ended prospect of the plains, the "eternal foreground" of the traveler whose end is not in sight and whose present opens up indefinitely ahead that is so difficult to bear. One turns away from such a prospect and looks to the past for familiar company and the certainty that one is not helpless and alone. Secularity understands and accepts what Dickens found to be an unbearable prospect: that nature and history both leave no lasting trace of the individual.

It is not easy, therefore, to draw a line between the present and the past, despite the cultural invention in the West of "the past." As Fabian (1983:73) points out, anthropologists seek to distinguish talking about the past from experiencing the presence of the past. This distinction underlies a certain contradiction between fieldwork and the reporting of one's observations to the anthropological community. On the one hand, in "the field," one enters into conversation in which both the anthropologist and the other are caught up in the same moment of time; they are truly contemporaries. In reporting such discussions to the anthropological community, however, the researcher is obligated to achieve a certain psychological and professional distance from these dialogues in the field. Instead of staying in the playful world of discourse in "the field," the anthropologist now must speak to the "field" of anthropology in a quite different voice, full of distance and detachment from the earlier engagements. In this distancing, the past is thus created: "The factum is that which *was* made or done, something that inevitably is 'past' in relation to the acts of recording, interpreting, and writing. In view of its obligations to facticity, how could there be any claims on anthropological discourse to heed the demands of coevalness qua copresence of talk and that which is talked about?" (Fabian 1983:73)

It would be quite different if the anthropologist, on returning to the professional world, could put on a play in which the discussions of the field, once illuminating and lively as well as taxing and occasionally abhorrent, could be dramatized. Such a play would transcend the movement from direct to indirect discourse: from engagement to reporting, from being a coproducer of a world large enough for two or more to inhabit to describing that world for others who were not and never will be there. The play would overcome the increasing social and psychological distance, as well as the indirection in language, that distinguishes the movement away from producing a world to reporting on it.

Thus, in this book I have adopted a similar strategy of using plays as a way of understanding the Western experience of time and particularly the chronic persistence of the past in the present. In a play, of course, one is entering vicariously into action that is being performed precisely because one is there to watch. Even in a good ethnographic interview in the field, of course, there is an element of performance; many of those being studied have already learned how to give a good interview. In a play, furthermore, one is watching a scene that presumably is being reenacted; the past is becoming present as one watches individual lives unfold in the theater as they presumably once unfolded on the stage of everyday life. Of course, there is a great deal of difference between attending one of these plays and talking about it, just as it is essential to learn how to draw the line between the present and the past. The past is thus present in these plays because it is being represented.

The past and the present are contemporaneous, however, not only because the actors and the audience are "coeval," in Fabian's sense of a time that is shared at least for the time being. There is another reason: many characters in these plays find it very difficult to transcend their own pasts. For some characters in these plays, indeed, there is little distinction between living in the past and talking about it. Neither the ethnographer nor the audience is watching a "tableau vivant," but they are engaged instead in producing a life together in which the past is reproduced in the present (see Fabian 1983:67).

To put it another way: some characters in these plays are scoring imaginary victories over time through fantasy, trying to make up for lost time, avoiding deadlines, and adopting busy schedules. Similarly, the play itself, by claiming to re-present what once took place, is dramatizing a partial and illusory transcendence over the passage of time. It is therefore going to be necessary to spoil the fun, so to speak, that is, to avoid entering uncritically into the illusion of being contemporary with the characters and the action. That is indeed a powerful illusion somewhat like daydreaming when one is sufficiently enchanted that one does not look at one's watch. The play, in this book, will be rather like a dramatization of an anthropologist's fieldwork. Because the characters are there to perform, as they also performed in "the field," the evidence is self-generated by the social system created by the social scientist and the "other." This contrivance, however, makes it especially suitable for the study of social systems that are themselves self-generated and self-referential; there is no hint of providence or of a transcendent viewpoint at work. These plays themselves, like the characters in them, are caught up in the irreversible and irrevocable passage of time.

This is not to say that one closes the door on fantasy or on the past, in the sense of denying, suppressing, or repressing feelings and memories. On the contrary, the truly secular person is capable of entertaining fantasy or memory without being displaced by them. An analogy to this state of mind might be the individual who attends the theater without becoming immersed in the play. One can examine the way the plot develops or the characters present themselves, or the way language is manipulated and certain effects are achieved, without being transported by the play and without becoming wholly identified with the characters. Thus, one would watch a play very much as Freud examined his dreams: for signs of earlier times, when his psyche had indeed been displaced by the dramas of everyday life.

A play, then, allows us to reenact, as though in the present, aspects of our past and of our own psyches, with which we would like to be familiar and yet from which we would like also to enjoy a little distance. We can therefore examine plays with the sort of depersonalized attention to ourselves that Freud achieved in *The Interpretation of Dreams*. The actors on stage move as if they are quite independent of us, and yet we recognize ourselves in them, for the time being, just as we discover ourselves in the characters in a dream who represent one or another aspect of our psyches. Even Freud found himself hiding behind—disguised as—various characters in his dreams. There is, then, a legitimate narcissistic interest in the play, one that is lacking, I would argue, in the larger society and its institutions. At least in the play we are entitled to imagine others like ourselves who are caught up in the flow of time. We—unlike the characters themselves—also know that the providence of the playwright is itself a contrivance.

A secular sense of time allows us to recover these lost identities, knowing that they are part of the past yet entering into them with the sympathies that only the present can muster. In the present, after all, we can understand the past as if it were a play, full of old passions, illusions, grandiosity, tantrums, self-defeating strategies for gaining affection and attention: in short, to borrow a term from Erasmus (1979:43–44), full of folly:

> Now the whole life of mortal men, what is it but a sort of play, in which various persons make their entrances in various costumes, and each one plays his own part until the director gives him his cue to leave the stage? Often he also orders one and the same actor to come on in different costumes, so that the actor who just now played the king in royal scarlet now comes on in rags to play a miserable servant. True, all these images are unreal, but this play cannot be performed in any other way.

Secularity understands that social life itself is based on "folly": a set of illusions that serve to keep people engaged with one another. Granted that some illusions are more self-serving or self-destructive than others and that some individuals are more ennobled than others by the fictions that bind them together in mutual antipathy. Erasmus does not scorn this drama, of course; as he points out, there is no "other way" to live with others than to share some responsibility for the drama and the fictions that allow social life to go on. It is important, as Erasmus (1979:44) goes on to say, "to overlook faults tolerantly" and not to spoil the party.

This distinction between appearance and reality, which turns social life into a mere play and makes it hard to take anyone, even the prince, too seriously, is based on the loss of the narcissistic illusion that the larger society does indeed somehow represent the self, holding the secret to one's individuality, and thus has a purchase on the psyche. However, there is nothing uniquely modern about the loss of this illusion. Mystics in every generation have understood that social life is a mere play of appearance and that their true selfhood resides elsewhere. As we shall see, Erasmus finally reveals himself as a mystic, who is fully aware of the divine in moments of ecstasy. For Erasmus, however, the experience of eternity was fleeting: momentary but also momentous, because it made every claim to reality and authority in this world seem to be part of a fool's play of appearances. It is not as if Erasmus were laying claim to a timeless grasp of the divine, so that experience of this world comes as a rude awakening. On the contrary, it is the fool's experience of a divine madness, a brief but transforming encounter with the other world, that is the rude awakening; this momentary ecstasy makes the present world seem to be something like a play, a bit dreamlike but still the only place to be. The fool's divine ecstasy, I will therefore argue, makes this world all the more obviously secular: apart from—and independent of—God, and real only on its own terms. It would henceforth be necessary to suffer fools gladly; as Marcel Gauchet (1997:77) puts it:

> Through their mystical union in Christ, the human and the divine were differentiated as the hierarchical intermixture of the earthly abode and the kingdom of heaven broke down into its basic constituents. . . . Christ evoked a difference that made any notions of radical escapism and deliverance from the here and now meaningless; in this life there was no escape from a world worthy of Christ's humanity."

That is what it meant to be a Christian fool: to live in this world on its own terms, without longing for deliverance and without a sense of superiority to any mortal, safe in the knowledge that one was in the company of fools, some of whom wore vestments and crowns and others of whom stood on far less ceremony and simply made out the best that they could.

To live in terms of the secular, then, is to know that all is "vanity," that what appears to transcend the passage of time is nothing more than a charade. Erasmus is clearly adopting a Christian viewpoint, not only when he suggests that it is important to suffer fools gladly but when he points to the folly of every way of life that makes a claim to transcendence. It is only folly, after all, that understands the things of the spirit and knows where true joys are to be found. Erasmus (1979:137) again: "So much beyond the body are the things of the spirit; things unseen, beyond what can be seen. This, indeed, is what the prophet promises: 'Eye has not seen, nor ear heard, nor has the heart of man conceived what things God has prepared for those who love him.' And this is Folly's part, which shall not be taken from her by the transformation of life, but shall be perfected."

Note the connections between ecstasy and the awareness of the fictitious or delusional aspects of social life. Long considered to be a demystifying aspect of critical social theory, the sense that social life is based on a conspiracy of silence about playacting has clear roots in Christian ecstasy. Pauline willingness to suffer fools more or less gladly stems from the larger sense of the folly of all this-worldly claims to transcendence.

Note also the leveling tendencies in Erasmus's (1979:116) notions about the folly of social distinction: "For if anyone thinks that happiness consists in gaining the favor of great rulers and living on familiar terms with those bejeweled and golden gods, what could be less helpful than wisdom?" Not only are the wise averse to success either in the Church or the state, they lack the enthusiasm for making money that distinguishes those in public office. More to the point, it takes a certain foolishness to endure the ceremonies or to seek the honors that make the social game worth playing: "Such foolishness as this creates states, it constitutes empires, civil offices, religion, counsels, judgments—in fact, human life is nothing more than an entertainment staged by folly" (Erasmus (1979:41). Stated thus flatly, Erasmus's view could be confused with any one of several modern voices arguing that narcissism—the desire to count for something and an inflated, unrealistic view of one's own potential are the engines that drive social life and make it seem serious. Social distinctions and the search for recognition are thus "folly" in the weaker, moralized sense of being based on existential anxiety and self-delusion; in that sense they—and the heart of social life—are "sinful." In Erasmus's (1979:136) view, however, the foolishness of everyday life is revealed not to the critics and the moralists who are infinitely serious about the weight of their own opinion but to those alone who have stepped apart from the stream of time if only for a moment— long enough to feel the temporal rush sweep away every distinction in its path, as they engage "in the pursuit of the eternal and invisible things of the spirit." For the rest, for his own critics in particular, Erasmus (1979:164) thought it better to abandon them to "the passing of time" than to try to win a battle on the field of academic honor.

It is this stepping out from—this ecstasy—that underlies not only the modern sense of social life as based on cultural fictions and self-deception but the willingness to play along as if it mattered. In the long run the mundane does matter; that is Erasmus's point. It is the place where the charades of everyday life and the pomp of high ceremony lose their distinction from one another, where the temporal and ecclesiastical lords seem as foolish as the local pundit in the bar who seeks to lord it over his fellow drinkers. In the twilight of folly all these social cats are more or less gray. If the pursuit of holiness leads one to see the world as folly, it is not so that one can then refuse to have anything to do with the world. Instead, it is so that one can accept its folly, suffer fools, and laugh at those who take themselves seriously, but without forgetting for a moment that, like Paul, one is also a quintessential fool. Christian faith allows one to let the secular world be secular without regret or longing, without estrangement or self-righteousness, as well as without the self-delusions of those whose titles and honor, money and ceremony allow them to feel that they themselves have stood apart from the mundane.

TWO

Secularization Reconsidered
Secret, Silent Mourning

THE SOCIAL LOCATION OF secularity is wherever social life is subject to radical uncertainty:

> The conditions of a system far from equilibrium are not time-reversible, in which it is sufficient to know the "law" and the initial conditions in order to predict its future states. Rather, *a system far from equilibrium is the expression of the "arrow of time," whose role is essential and constructive. In such a system, the future is uncertain and the conditions are irreversible.* The laws that we can formulate therefore enumerate only possibilities, never certainties."[1]

In a secular social system, the future is unpredictable and each moment may bring something new. Secularity is thus the experience of radical uncertainty: radical because the ultimate may be at stake—life and death—even in circumstances that seem quite ordinary; and uncertain because there are no laws that give one a reliable guide on how to think, feel, or act.[2] Now the social order itself, the state and the larger society, is itself too open and complex, too subject to uncertainty and change, to maintain the trappings of transcendence over time. Thus, the ideology of transcendence, whether based on an appeal to providence or to irresistible historical forces, no longer "works" because it does not fit either the conditions or the experience of modern societies.

A providential sense of history once linked the person's encounter with grief and death to the sentiments of folk, communal, familial, civic, and national sentiment. In the midst of an increasingly strenuous and exacting public and corporate schedule, individuals are now increasingly left to the solitude of their own experiences of significant moments, intractable loss, haunting memory, and of anxiety about the future. As grief becomes an increasingly solitary affair, so does the individual's experience of time. Whether the individual's grief is retroactive and anticipatory as well as of the moment, individuals are increasingly bereft of an overarching providential conviction that links personal and public loss to a divine plan or historical tendency. Secularity lacks a collectively accepted destination and recognizes only the private end of each individual in death.

Secularity also entails the experience of a radical disjunction between personal and public time. The individual is no longer protected from the onslaught—or slow passage—of time by the institutions that, like barrier reefs, have provided something of a sheltered harbor for the individual. If one is to find tranquility, it will not be in the absence of the waves of time that continue to flow over the person; they are still relentless and inexorable.

The celebrated deaths of figures like John F. Kennedy and Martin Luther King, Mother Teresa and Princess Diana, remind us that grief is a leveling emotion that therefore has long had political implications. Grief has forged ties of solidarity that cross the widest of social divisions, but it can also tear a nation apart. On a smaller scale, grief has brought communities together at moments of sacred recollection and enabled those with the most intense emotions to experience them not only in private but in the midst of public display that either leveled or intensified social distinctions. On the whole, however, these collective outpourings are remarkable for their irregularity. The consummation of grief at the death of Diana was especially surprising to the British themselves and suggested the existence of a huge reservoir of private emotion that had not been drained by collective rites.

In secularized societies, individuals manage their losses and face death on their own terms; grief is no longer the center of communal activity and is increasingly a private affair. With few exceptions, the rhythms of individuals' lives, from birth to death, go by without the benefit of institutional rites or public ceremony. There are few public occasions on which to note such critical moments as a miscarriage or stillbirth, the loss of a job, or the entrance of the individual into a nursing home. In a secular society, therefore, individuals are increasingly left to their own devices to manage their own existential anxiety.

The more secular a society becomes, the more does the subjective experience of time become plastic. To be sure, certain holidays like Thanksgiving or Easter may continue to shape the experience of time before and after the day itself in ways that powerfully affect both expectation and memory. One's own sense of when to die may well be affected by the anticipation of important holidays and by the experience of their aftermath. One does not want to be late for a day like Christmas.

There was a time when private grief and public mourning were more closely aligned with each other. For instance, nearly three centuries ago Giambattista Vico was commissioned to write inscriptions in honor of the Empress Eleanor to be placed over her tomb. He composed a tribute to be inscribed over the door of a royal chapel dedicated to Eleanor that concluded with the injunction: "Your Prince, Delight of the State / is in mourning / Hither do you, O citizens / bring your tribute of public mourning" (Vico 1944:176). Not only was the prince's grief publicized; the people were called upon to make the tribute of mourning. Thus, mourning bound the people and prince in a community of grief and recollection.

The communal and public nature of grief was the result of earlier stages in the process of secularization. In the first "age," according to Vico (1944:169), cultures were dominated by gods, and "families were ruled by sovereign princes under the government of the gods, ordering all human affairs according to the divine auspices." It was a "divine" age in which Oriental gods moved westward and took on Greek and Latin names, and language was hieroglyphic rather than alphabetic. The sorrows of the gods were the subject of ballad and epic; not so the grief of ordinary mortals. Vico's (1944:170) next age was one of heroes, and its language was metaphoric and thus suitable for governments of "heroic kingdoms or ruling orders of notables." These may have been warrior brotherhoods, and they laid the foundations of civil government not only through force but through law. In this age we can see a concerted attempt to involve the people in the veneration of noble ancestry. For instance, Augustus ensured that every ward in the city of Rome had a shrine in which his own ancestors were honored. Thus, the household of the emperor was expanded to receive the devotion of the citizens. However, this democratization of respect for the dead did not extend far beyond the precincts of Rome, except where Roman rule imposed prayers for the Emperor and his family on client priesthoods (Beard et al. 1998:184ff.).

In these inscriptions Vico realizes a vision of the modern age, or *saeculum*, as the one that is truly open, egalitarian, and secular. The third age was "of common men and vernacular languages, [and it] coincides with the times of ideas of a human nature completely developed and hence recognized as identical in all men" (Vico 1944: 171–72). Thus in the inscription over the royal chapel, Vico identified the mourning of the prince with the grief of the people. The old mysteries that separated the nobility from the people are gone; there is common language, a vernacular, so-called because of its origin among the plebeians. There are no longer two cities at war with one another, one noble, the other vulgar, but one in which law levels the differences between the weak and the powerful. It is the time of "popular commonwealths, which are naturally open, generous, and magnanimous (being commanded by the multitude, who naturally understand natural equity" (Vico 1984:350).

Of course, Vico's (1984:351) notion of a secularizing process in history is clearly ideological, since history culminates in monarchies that alone can "make the powerful and the weak equal before the law." However, the monarchy has become democratized and wisdom become the custom of the people themselves. Not only is the prince's mourning no longer secret; the people of the city are called upon to stand before the tomb and to give vent to a grief that is both popular and princely. Even the tomb itself is open and empty, an emblem of the consummation of history in an age without secrets or mystery. The empty tomb, originally the Christian symbol for the new age, has become the secular reality.

There is an eternal foundation, however, for Vico's secular monarchy. Vico (1944:171) has no doubt about the progress of history or its end: "[M]onarchies are the final governments in which nations come to rest." Moreover, although there is a single human nature binding the princes and the peoples, and law arises "among the nations," it still must be perfected by a reason that in turn employs "the maxims of an eternal justice" (Vico 1944:172).

For Vico there will be no separation between private grief and public mourning. Individuals will not be left to their own devices to assuage their losses; no one faces death on his or her own. Indeed, this was one of the great victories of an earlier age, when the plebeians of Rome were brought into the body politic by being allowed to marry and thus to create a legacy that would be recognized by law. In Vico's view, secularization gives the people their share of aristocratic victories over time.

The process of secularization was for Vico (1984:104) clearly providential in origin: "[T]hese institutions have been established by divine providence . . . [in] an ideal eternal history traversed in time by the history of every nation in its rise, development, maturity, decline, and fall." Individuals, then, in their own paths through time would contribute to this eternal but historic process. Consider, for instance, Vico's memorial to the Empress Eleanor. In one part of the inscription, to be placed inside the royal chapel over one of its arches, Vico (1944:177) wrote: "With tears o citizens let your most earnest vows be offered that the spirit of Eleanor received in heaven may obtain by divine favor an offering for the Emperor Charles from Her Imperial Highness Elizabeth such as she herself gave to Leopold so that she may not leave the Christian world in grief for her forever unassuaged." Here the traffic between heaven and earth remains uninterrupted by death and the passage of time. The prayers of the people will have an effect on the spirit of Eleanor in heaven, as Eleanor, in turn, will intercede on behalf of the people. Through her intercession her son Charles VI of Austria will have in his turn a son who, like Charles himself, is an incarnation of Empress Eleanor's noble spirit. Thus, the legacy of the spirit remains unbroken by death from one generation to the next, and the living, by their prayers, strengthen the souls of the departed. It is not a strange sentiment in a Catholic country that has long been schooled in the disciplines of purgatory or in a traditional society that knows an unbroken spiritual succession over the generations. Public and private piety are joined in acts of mourning and intercession, and the individual is given institutional shelter from the ravages of time.

The individual's experience of time is now largely divorced from a larger, communal rhetoric that would link the dead with the living, but the world of which Vico wrote survived in some places at least into the nineteenth century in France. There millions still believed in purgatory as a place for the departed to make up for lost time. That belief, moreover, was caught up in other devotions: the pieties of the family at the graveside, folk religion and its preoccupation with the return of the dead, and civic and national ceremonies that enshrined the dead in public memory. Even now, writes Thomas Kselman (1993:214), in his study of death in nineteenth-century France, "the civil religion of twentieth century France owes much to the cultivation of a sentimental attachment to the dead that had developed around family tombs in the nineteenth century." It is an attachment that was deepened and solemnized by the rites of a church that continued to believe that the living could relieve the burdens of the souls of the departed in purgatory, a belief that cemented the ties between the living and the dead not only with affectionate and pious memory but with the bonds of eternal obligation.

Even those who decried ecclesiastical and civic ritual still believed in the public significance of the moment of death as a time for moral reflection. Kselman (1993:213) notes that even when popular belief in the doctrine of purgatory began to wane, still visits to the local cemetery embodied a more secularized devotion to the memory of the dead:

> The call for the living to pray for the dead is related instead to the desire to remember. Despite doubts about the Catholic model of the afterlife, this association between praying and remembering has endured and become a central characteristic of the visit to the cemetery. . . .
>
> Cemeteries were centers for family shrines, places where the living and the dead could be united. The feelings of community and solidarity evoked in the cemeteries could also be extended to the village and the city as a whole, and used to link local sentiments with the French nation.

The process of secularization may undermine the usual religious or civic rites that transform moments into the sacred, but a tendency to enshrine these moments persists even in the vacuum left by the failure of public ceremony. In his discussion of "the cult of death" Kselman (1993:291–302) describes in some detail the critical reaction to a painting by Courbet, the *Burial at Ornans;* it is a painting that displays a wide range of reactions immediately prior to the start of a graveside ceremony. While the priest finds his place in the prayer book, some bystanders clearly grieve, while others turn away from the scene, are distracted, or are simply as disengaged as a local dog that is presented in the usual place at the lower right hand corner of the painting, diametrically opposite the cross. Kselman (1993:301) observes: "Looking at the *Burial*, the viewer knows that the proper ceremonies are about to take place, but Courbet suggests that they will be momentary and artificial rather than deeply, personally, and lastingly felt. He thus adheres to and in a perverse way expresses the nineteenth century's high standards of personal belief." Even skeptics and secularists would agree, Kselman goes on to note, that "the last moments" are inherently solemn and definite even for those who do not believe in the Church's authority to enshrine them in its own sacred mysteries. There is both depiction and critique in Courbet's painting of the burial.

The aura of the temporal displaces the everlasting, and Courbet conveys the sense that any attempt to enshrine the moment will be contrived and short-lived. No doubt that many of the French were ambivalent about this development: critical of the Church's claims to represent the sacred and yet opposed to the commercialization of death and any attempt to trivialize domestic affection or to suggest that the family itself could not transcend death and the passage of time. The sheer moment, unadorned by devotion or affection, piety or any trace of a higher morality, was too profane (Kselman (1993: 301–2). Life on the level of the purely momentary would be no better than that of the dog, depicted, like some of the mourners themselves, looking elsewhere.

It would be difficult for the modern state to engage individual piety so directly. Individuals in a society such as the contemporary

United States may still have a common language, although that varies by the local community and is subject to political debate, but they live in too many different circumstances to share a sense of common fate. Not even the churches are able to articulate a moral discourse that is binding on the nation as a whole. Rather, the churches have become a congeries of interest groups fighting among themselves for shreds of political influence; none is capable of proposing a moral agenda for the nation as a whole without being immediately reduced to the status of a quite particular and partial interest group by the religious opposition.

Beyond the generations that may encounter each other within a single family, there seems to be little common sense of responsibility either to the past or to the future: "[T]hose alive today can feel entirely impervious to the sanctions and moral reproach of future generations" (Offshe 1996:47). Different groups have different ancestors, whose sufferings remain to be assuaged by public policy; there is no common ancestral pool (e.g., slaves in Egypt) from which to draw political and spiritual inspiration for the future. To evoke the grandchildren as a generation that will stand in judgment on the present cohort of politicians and moral leaders may have some rhetorical appeal, but that appeal does not produce consensus on what to do about taxation, social security, the environment, capital savings and investment, or national defense.

Not only have time horizons become short for the larger society with its major institutions and corporations, but individuals are left to their own devices to remember and imagine over the sweep of time. While they may draw spiritual inspiration from ancient saints or gurus and while they may imagine a day of millennial rapture in some undefined future, or even enter imaginatively into other "parallel universes," they do so without the promise of any inscription over their tomb that evokes collective mourning and anticipation.

Less enmeshed in any single milieu, individuals now offer themselves in a variety of contexts, from home to work, in voluntary organizations or chains of command, each of which has its own identity, sense of purpose, schedules and calendars, and temporal horizons. Their pieties are increasingly voluntary and may be quite singular; their conversions are seldom public, and entire communities no longer shout their devotion in a single act of collective adoration. Time, with its passage, its rhythms, its occasions of loss or of wonder, and its inevitable end in death, is increasingly experienced by the individual as his or her private affair, whereas companies and churches, political parties and the government, sports and the entertainment industry compete with one another for control over the days and hours of work and leisure. A final time, a day of general accounting, or communal days of repentance and atonement, of memory and anticipation, no longer collect and galvanize the whole nation or community, and they engage individuals in only one aspect of their social life.[3]

To be sure, there are still millions of millennialists and apocalypticists whose visions of the Rapture are convincing to themselves, but they do not enthrall those other millions who regard history as a continuous and open-ended progress from the relatively primitive to the relatively developed. Of course, there are still millions who expect a divine providence to provide a dramatic or fulfilling close to history, while there are others, equally numerous and convinced, who regard the end as quite open, undetermined, and perhaps never to be seen by humankind. It is this latter tendency that I regard as a sign of secularization, and in this book it is with their experience of time that I am primarily concerned.

THREE

The Loss Of A Temporal Matrix

W E HAVE BEEN EXPLORING THE paradox that Christianity is partly responsible for the loss of a sense of providence and historical necessity in modern societies. Not only has the Church uprooted and eradicated deviant local pieties; the Christian God has been relentlessly transcendent above every institution and community. The effect, as Marcel Gauchet (1997:95) has recently reminded us, has been to deprive tradition and the social order of their sacred trappings; they emerge clearly visible in the light of a human day. Now humanity is to own and control, adapt and construct social institutions to suit its own wants and purposes:

> As God withdrew, the world changed from something *presented* as unalterable   to something to be *constituted*. God having become Other to the world, the world now became Other to humans, in two ways: by its objectivity at the level of representation, and by its ability to be transformed at the level of action. . . . And if he ["man"] entered into a relation of otherness, it was within and according to a defined goal, namely to realize his ontological independence. (Gauchet 1997:95; Gauchet's emphasis).

Humans are no longer to revere their institutions but to use them; no longer are the stars and the elements to be considered divine emblems of a world beyond us but the matter from which humans can shape not only themselves but their own material universe. Gauchet (1997:203) once more:

> When the gods abandon the world, when they stop coming to no-
> tify us of their otherness to it, the world itself begins to appear
> other, to disclose an imaginary depth that becomes the object of a
> special quest, containing its purpose and referring only to itself.

To live in the secular world, then, is to take the world on its own terms. It is this world, not some other, that holds the secrets behind our own existence. Bereft of the shelter of institutions that transcend the passage of time, individuals have to seize their own times; time is indeed all they have. No matter how often the president of the United States postures among schoolchildren or in the ruins of various disasters, the fact remains that the state follows the calendar of the tax year, the fiscal year, and the election year. Individuals are on their own to sort out their existential questions and to become confident of their own being-in-time. The world is becoming increasingly impersonal: not only a matter of fact, but a matter of time.

The individual can take less narcissistic comfort from a society whose institutions have become attuned to their own official calendars and priorities rather than to the personal rhythms of life and death, of growth and hope, of loss and final abandonment. Individuals are on their own to face the passage of time. Even the bureaucracy of the churches, which used to mediate guarantees for the soul, is nearly as rational and impersonal as the state. It is up to the individual, therefore, to embark on the quest for salvation without the benefit or hindrance of clergy. What once was understood to be the freedom of the Christian has become widespread, if not universal.

Such freedom is demanding and produces more than a little existential anxiety. As Gauchet (1997:165) later puts it, "It is an immense problem to establish your identity when it is no longer given by others and, strange though it may sound, an even greater problem to conform to yourself when you are released from your allegiance to the gods." It is not surprising that individuals have therefore been seeking to protect themselves from the erosion of time by imagining themselves represented by immortal institutions like the nation or the state. It is easier to invent cultural fictions like the "civil religion" than it is to take responsibility for constructing the world. It is easier to imagine one-self the bearer of timeless virtues and vitality in an immortal nation than to take responsibility for one's own self-definition and salvation.

Paradoxically, the Church has been a primary source of the impulse toward secularity precisely because it tried to mediate the grace of a God who transcends all forms of mediation, a point superbly made by Gauchet. In his view, the Church bears witness that "there could be no other conceivable conjunction between the Natural and the Supernatural" than Jesus Christ's life and death (Gauchet 1997: 137). For Gauchet (1997:137), it is a witness that undermines the Church's—and all other institutions'—claims to embodying the transcendent: "Ecclesiastical mediation was thus built on something that cast doubt on the very possibility of mediation."

For centuries, Gauchet (1997:135) argues, the contradiction between Christian freedom and the Church's own claim to provide access to the transcendent has created a dynamic tension in Western society—a chronic impulse away from ecclesiastical authority and toward the direct, unmediated access of the inner self to the God who is above all gods: "The explosive paradox of spiritual subjugation is that it legitimates a direct appeal by believers, over the system's head and over its administrators, to the ultimate source of all justice and reason. The bureaucracy of belief could not work without tacitly recognizing the autonomy of conscience." Christianity thus has sown the seeds of the Church's own self-destruction as the mediator of a providential viewpoint. There may be an "ultimate source of all justice and reason," a providence that oversees human history and the fate of individuals. At the very least, however, individuals do not have to go through the Church to get access to that providence; they are in that sense on their own. In the same way, the Church sets up a court of final appeal above its own head, to whom individuals suppressed by the Church can turn for comfort and recognition; this again undermines the Church's attempt to mirror what it claims to be the lasting, even eternal aspects of the individual psyche. By the Gospels' own account, individuals do not need to seek their own spiritual reflection in the institution of the Church.

This freedom may be heady, but it also brings with it the burden of time. The awareness of the passage of time makes every one, in the end, marginal; one's existence is precarious, and one's individuality dispensable. No wonder that secularity requires a struggle of the soul against the psyche's own tendency to circumscribe, to screen out or even dispel the knowledge of one's own temporality. To be open to the flood of time, one has to enter the depths of one's own psyche: the world of underground memory in which moments last with a vitality that seems to defy the passage of time itself. In the same depths one encounters deep defenses against the experience of time, anesthetics against loss and disappointment, dread of departure and of being forever late: the markers, so to speak, of mortality in the soul. Such a radical openness to inner uncertainty and mystery, however, is precisely what one would expect of a Christian tradition that has long exalted a God whose ways are not the ways of humans and who is forever "hid in light inaccessible." As Gauchet (1997:137) puts it: "For if God is truly the other, inexhaustibly different, in his supreme wisdom, from what we manage to understand of him, then we can only accommodate the enigmatic, disturbing surplus of meaning deep in our hearts."

Secularity no longer thrives on a defensive reaction to the claims of the Church or—for that matter—of the state or any other institution to mediate something transcendent and even divine. We live in an era of disintermediation, in which individuals have direct access to the divine, just as they have direct access to the markets and can bypass the local bank and the broker.[1] Similarly, the churches have lost their monopoly on the sacred, and individuals have access to a wide range of sources of religious inspiration and comfort whether or not they ever attend church. Those who do attend frequently make up their own minds as to what to believe, and many withhold the tokens of allegiance associated with church membership and denominational identification. In the range of cultural options open to the public, the churches occupy an increasingly small niche in the marketplace for meaning.

Gauchet is writing with a full awareness of the spiritual depths that have opened up in a century of Freudian thought and exploration. Of course, neither Gauchet nor Freud himself was a Freudian; the point is that a full range of meaning is available to those who explore the depths of their own psyches and find there a mystery—as

Gauchet puts it—"a surplus of meaning" formerly anchored in divine transcendence. To live in the world on any other terms is drastically to reduce that surplus of meaning and to falsify that mystery: to impose a text, as it were, on silence and utter complexity.

Secularity, then, is the willingness to submit to the radical experience of the passage of time. That requires, to begin with, that one be wholly open to what Gauchet calls the "surplus of meaning." Such openness is possible because of a God who is utterly transcendent and whose ways are entirely not our ways. However, that same transcendence makes a providential view of history problematical, at least in any form administered by the Church or the state. That same transcendence also ensures that individuals will find no immediate institutional or societal reflection of their convictions and commitments. There is an insult to one's narcissism and a challenge to one's basic trust in the universe inherent in this faith; one is left, so to speak, to the mercies of time.

In a secular society, time is increasingly what some ecclesiastical quarters call "ordinary time" precisely because it is not shaped to fit into the framework of ritual or does not contain days of solemn obligation. In a secularized society, these mundane or ordinary times may then seem to be rather insignificant; indeed, one may feel as if one continues to miss critical moments and is thus perennially running "late." A religious tradition may seek to capture this tendency to enshrine the moment by sanctifying the memory of crucial founding events, as in the spiritual "Were You There When They Crucified My Lord?" However, this hallowing may also cause the believer to feel in retrospect as if he or she failed to rise to such an important occasion. Indeed, churches may exploit this tendency especially on days like Good Friday, in which the believer is sometimes cast in the role of a disciple who failed to watch with Christ during his moment of trial or who, like Peter, denied allegiance and deserted the scene. Thus, to be late may mean that one has failed to seize the moment.[2]

Secular time may seem to go by in discrete little drops: a little here, and a little there. This experience of time is familiar to prisoners, for whom the passage of time is like the slow dropping water from a faucet, moment by moment. One thinks of the so-called Chinese water torture as a metaphor for this experience of the painfully slow passage of time in discrete, unrelated, and empty moments. It is therefore not surprising to find that some people yearn for the passage of time to speed up and imagine that a day of release will be soon forthcoming. Apocalyptic imagination, I would suggest, is often fed by an experience of time that is slow, empty of meaning, and torturous. One can feel as if one is running late simply because one expects an end to come that is constantly being postponed.

In a highly secular society, someone's experience of time may seem to stretch indefinitely from the present into the past and into the future. The present may then seem like a very long but indefinite span, as if one were "doing time" or "doing a stretch." As I have already noted, on his travels through America Dickens spoke of the "eternal foreground," when the present seemed to go on forever and the horizon kept receding. Sometimes it seems as if the future will never begin, and the long stretch of the present becomes virtually unendurable. Of course, experiencing time as elastic, a person may feel as if the present hardly lasts long enough and is so fleeting as to seem virtually unreal.

The secular experience of time is not only plastic and elastic; it is also contingent on a number of factors. Much depends on how far one is projecting oneself forward or backward and on whether one feels inwardly certain of one's own being. Those with a tenuous sense of their own being and who try to imagine themselves in the future may be afflicted with doubts as to whether they will arrive (i.e., as to whether they will "be there"). Similarly, those whose sense of themselves is fragile and who look backward, may find that they have little to show for themselves; they might feel "late," like someone who has undergone the social death suffered by prisoners and patients. Whether time is felt to flow more or less speedily, for instance, or continuously rather than in unrelated, discrete moments, or to be full rather than empty may also depend on how a person experiences a particular task or a situation (Friedman 1990:19ff.).

It is sometimes argued that less secularized societies may construe time in ways that are more cyclical than linear. "What goes around comes around," and it is as if the circle of time repeats itself annually. Such societies reenact the past in ways that allow the individual to imagine that one can make up for lost time. The more secular societies stretch time into a continuous and linear duration in which every moment and every day is unrepeatable. Under these conditions time is always quite literally being lost.

Of course, the distinction between cyclical and linear time has served ideological purposes for distinguishing modern from so-called traditional or primitive societies; it is a distinction that does not hold up well under close analysis of the various ways in which time is construed and experienced in everyday life (Gell 1992:92; Adam 1995:34ff.). Individuals in "modern" societies can experience time in ways that seem primitive; one may be enjoying the cyclical repetition of annual holidays and yet be worried about the end of a fiscal year. Similarly, those in pre-industrial societies can experience time in ways that seem quite "modern." In any society, one can feel late simply because it is difficult simultaneously to live up to the expectations embedded in a variety of calendars that operate concurrently.

In this book I am suggesting that individuals increasingly experience time in ways that are "out of synch" with the world of work and politics; the professions and the public have their own ways of marking time, but these are less and less symbolic of the ways that individuals actually experience time in their everyday lives. Certainly one may experience a moment, a time, as being intensely serious without having that experience acknowledged or synchronized in any ritual, ceremony, calendar, or other public event. The momentous for the individual may be uneventful for the larger society, just as the eventful for the larger society may seem to be of no moment whatsoever for the individual. Individuals have existential anxieties that fail to show up on the schedule of appointments in the doctor's office; groups have memories of old tragedy that fail to show up in public calendars; communities have fears of the future that are not noted in the plans of policy makers. Under these conditions the sacred is vastly reduced in scope, and societies increasingly lose their ability to forge the institutions necessary for trust, commitment, or even sacrifice. The larger society itself and its major institutions do not embody the history of the people, enshrine collective memory, offer a place for individuals to be memorialized, guarantee a lifetime of care or employment, or offer a purchase on the future. As a result, Western societies are undergoing a fundamental shift in the relation of the innermost self to the larger society. Because the temporal paths of the larger society are increasingly secular, individuals are left to a temporal world of personal memory and private imagination. The individual's existential sense of time has less and less to do with the time frames offered by the larger society.

No wonder, then, that the public outpouring of grief at the death of Diana took clergy, the politicians and the royal family itself by surprise and that pundits searched for precedent in a variety of relatively awkward places. What was emerging on the streets of London had been there all the time, as individuals had long been facing their own losses and limitations, their own mourning and sadness, without the benefit of public ceremony and recognition.

Who is to say whether Diana's life was—or was not—in keeping with the forms of royalty, of good taste, of public decorum? Were her celebrated clothes spoofs of royal dress or in keeping with a slightly more flamboyant expression of excellence? Should her brother, the earl, have included in his remarks a clear criticism of the royal family, or was he in fact paying proper deference to the royalty of his sister that required no official sanction but only the tribute of the people who had made her their own princess? In their intense coverage of Diana, were the media in fact mediating the center to the periphery or were they creating the virtual Diana for whom the public engaged in virtual mourning? The questions underscore Claus Offshe's remarks about the "transitoriness," the "innovation," and the temporal instability of modern societies.

> The sphere of cultural norms and values as well as of aesthetic criteria of validity are also subject to an equally pervasive proclivity toward transitoriness and innovation. In the modernization process, traditional monopolies of interpretation, claims to absoluteness, and doctrinal compulsions become obsolete, and accordingly the orienting norms of the sciences, of occupation, leisure, art, family, sexuality, religion, education, etc., become variable, subject to choice, and unstable over time. (1996:7)

This lack of reliable norms and ceremonies for public grief allows personal experiences with time to become increasingly "out of synch" with the times of the public sphere. The English social anthropologist Barbara Adam (1995:52–3) argues that "the pervasive feeling of time running out" is due to the incompatibility of "clock-time" (by which she means highly rationalized forms of social management and control) and "the embedded, creative and constitutive times of life" (by which she means the ordinary experiences of families and communities). The "times" in which individuals live out their loves and hatreds, their losses and their reunions, now radically diverge from the public sense of calendrical and official time, and this split has important consequences not only for individual aspiration and grief but for one's sense of having a solitary selfhood and a personal destiny that separates one from the fate of clan and community, church and nation.

Of course, societies less coordinated by the clock than the contemporary West also have had a number of abstract and formal conceptions of time; indeed, some quite traditional and agrarian societies are driven by time pressures (see Friedman 1990:110; Gell 1992: 84ff.). These also may have conflicted with the existential experience of time in everyday life. Thus Westerners are not the only ones to reduce public time to an abstraction while enchanting everyday experiences of time with memory and apprehension.[3] Nor are other cultures more prone than the West to turn time into a fetish.[4]

When the sacred is no longer able through public ritual to solemnize the individual's experience of time, the theater provides a way to dramatize that experience. The plays of the English dramatist David Hare provide us with a number of interesting dramatizations of the incommensurate nature of public and personal time. In *The Absence of War,* for instance, Hare opens and closes the play with a moment of silence during an event of national mourning for the dead. In the opening scene we are reminded that the dead in the wars of this century would stretch in a line, four abreast, from London to Edinburgh: a vision that creates a nearly unbearable foreground in which the present stretches backward into a past filled with the dead. During the requisite two-minute silence a character on stage, known as Andrew, tells the audience that he loves the silence because it enables him to question the busyness, the overscheduled days, the ridiculous hours, and the chronic concern for being at a meeting that one is "already late for." Andrew says that he has a "theory": "People of my age, we did not fight in a war. If you fight in a war, you have some sense of personal worth. So now we seek it by keeping busy. We work and hope we will feel we do good" (Hare 1993:2). It is easier to feel that one is running late in the race to meet deadlines and keep appointments than it is to face death or to remember the dead. It is also easier to feel that one is in danger of missing a deadline than it is to anticipate one's own death. It is easier to be late for appointments than it is to be "late" in the mortal sense.

Postponed grieving turns into anticipatory grief. Fears of abrupt change in the future take the place of departures in the past that have been too sudden or painful to be fully endured. An old disaster becomes a dreaded apocalypse. Former losses turn into fears that one will be too late for some departure in the future. Anticipatory grief takes many forms, but it shows up most frequently, I will argue, in a preoccupation with schedules, departures, and deadlines.

Preoccupation with deadlines, of course, may also be a symptom of the individual's dread at facing the prospect of death. Like any symptom, deadlines not only symbolize the disease but perpetuate it. Returning to Hare's play, *The Absence of War*, we find Andrew on the staff of a Labour politician named George Jones, who is the party's leading candidate for prime minister in a forthcoming election. Jones himself faces various deadlines and somehow keeps failing to meet them. At the end of the play, Jones tells us why he has so much trouble facing the end; he had been unutterably grieved by his mother's death in the war. In her absence, and in the absence of that war, he remains interminably busy and forever late. Jones's closing speech occurs in a moment of national silence for the men who have died in the wars of the twentieth century. In an aside to the audience, Jones confides his reason for being at a loss for words: "My own mother died. She died in an air-raid. In South London, during the blitz. It's almost my very first memory, my aunts weeping as they gave me the news. And since then . . . fifty years' honest endeavor. Fifty years doing my best. Being told everything I love and value no longer meets the needs of the day" (p. 109). Jones loses his mother and is thus perennially out of synchrony with his own times. As for the future, it is difficult for Jones to project himself forward. While he prides himself on being able to "pull the trigger" or "do the deed," he has more private and morose moments in which he reflects on his sacrifices. "It would hardly be worth it. To have sacrificed everything. If at the end you were just going to lose" (p. 40). His life is one of anticipatory grief, disguised as a tendency always to be late, a fear of taking risks, and an unwillingness to sacrifice.

For the bereft, the world offers only the prospect of more losses. It is difficult for Jones to project himself forward into the future or to see himself as having arrived. His aides say of Jones that he has problems with knowing how facts are supposed to cohere and in judging how long he has to go. When one has failed to put old losses to rest and is thus dreading the future, the world itself seems impermanent, chancy, and incoherent, and even one's own soul may not seem very real or solid. Referring at the end of the play to his failure to beat the Tories in the election, Jones finally confesses: "In the year since my own bruising experience I have found myself asking a question which will always haunt us and to which no easy answer appears ... Is this history? Is everything history? Could we have done more? Was it possible? And how shall we know?" (p. 109–10)

The question of whether we could have done more—like the question "Was it possible?—suggests a profound vagueness about limits. Not to endure fully a sudden and brutal loss, like the wartime death of Jones's mother, is to postpone knowing that one's life, as one knows it, has come to an end; the future will not be like the past, and the one for whom one is searching will not be there. To continue to search for someone who will always be found to have been missing is to anticipate grief rather than to experience it fully. It is easier to ask whether one could have done more than to face the fact that there is nothing more to be done.

No wonder, then, that Jones acts as if he could always have done more. Jones's aides worry about the fact that, while the man is "dynamite," he seldom comes across. His speeches end up in a verbal "freefall," like the British pound. Early in life he was powerfully eloquent; now he seems to have lost the courage of his convictions. He goes into the House, starts on a strong note, and then eventually begins to stumble. He ends up by being at a loss for words. On the occasion of one of his hapless speeches, Jones complains that he could not think of "how to end it." His complaint is revealing. It is indeed the ending that he cannot adequately face: the end of the question, the end of the speech, the end of the election campaign, the final contest, the end of his own life.

Jones is always at a loss for words when it comes to the end. Always late, always keeping people waiting, always seeking time out, he cannot bear to be realistic about his chances for failure at the end of the campaign. There is destruction ahead that he cannot face, and so he anesthetizes himself with moments of transfiguring beauty. The play suggests that the losses at the end of Jones's career were rooted in the loss of his mother during the war, but that remains a secret to the end. The public time, marked by the election, is apparently quite divorced from the existential time in which Jones lives, swamped with memory and burdened by his imagination of a deadline that he can never meet.

A life of anticipatory grief thus dooms one to recapitulate earlier losses, even while the larger society is operating on a relentless, linear push into the future. Of course, Jones is not wholly out of touch with time in the public sphere. Before Jones knows that Parliament is about to be dissolved and an election to be called, he nonetheless senses that "we're running out of time. We need someone soon" (p. 19). However, this sense of time is due to his chronic sense of anticipated loss, and it fails to precipitate timely action on Jones's part. His aides, especially the women, are loath to tell him the truth, and he therefore hires a new member of his staff, a woman named Lindsay, who tries her best to tell him how he is really doing in the public's estimation. Remember that it was Jones's aunts who brought him the bad news of his mother's death.

Jones's private and chronic sense of grief thus makes it hard for him to accept and grasp the rhythms of time in the public sphere of politics, of daily life, of busy schedules, and of approaching deadlines. It is therefore left to Jones's staff to remind him that he could always be doing more, that time is indeed running out, and that loss is inevitable if he does not act decisively, but Jones seems unable to see the whole picture. Two men on Jones's staff have tried without success to convince him that he has a problem in seeing the connection between one fact and another; there is something incoherent about Jones's view of the world around him. In fact, Jones goes on too long in his speeches and does not get closure. Conversely, when an interviewer on television showed that Jones had a weak grasp of the facts about social security, Jones had backtracked "interminably" (p. 32). That is just it. For Jones, because the end is always dreaded but forever out of sight, he looks endlessly backward.

Hare's characters repeatedly fail precisely because they keep backtracking. Many of his characters have made unsatisfying attachments to a career or to lovers and spouses; these attachments are supposed to offer them support, but instead they become a source of torment. Thus Hare's characters seek to make up for lost time by recovering old sources of satisfaction and by renewing old attachments. These techniques for making up for lost time inevitably prolong their suffering rather than relieve it. Finally, the end of these attachments often comes abruptly and as a surprise, even when it was foreseen. Unresolved grief inevitably produces self-inflicted losses and self-defeat. For instance, the inability to make satisfying connections and backward-looking attempts to preserve them inevitably make one tardy in responding to the demands of the moment. In *The Absence of War*, Jones, although he is the party's candidate for leader, is taken by surprise when Kendrick, the Tory prime minister, "goes down the mall," that is, goes to the palace to submit his resignation and to declare a new election. Everyone in Jones's group is surprised. They had spent years preparing for the next election, but it is a race that they had not expected to come so soon: after Christmas, maybe, but not now, while the Tories were trailing Labour by six percentage points in the polls.

"Backtracking" also makes it difficult to imagine how one will sustain the self in the protracted and indefinite present. In Parliament, Jones had accused the government of being like "a lonely drunk wandering through the streets at four-thirty in the morning, muttering to itself, blaming its misfortunes on others and desperately searching, scrabbling through the early morning trashcans for any political ideas it might still be able to lift." The question is, "How long? . . . Please tell us how long?" (p. 11). Jones's question, "How long?" alarms the prime minister, who asks the queen to dissolve Parliament and declare a new election because he can not stand the negativity any more, and the country needs confidence in its government.

Jones is taken by surprise that the end of this government and the longed-for battle should come so soon. When asked whether he expected the election to be declared, he responds, "Of course not. No. I'd booked for *Hamlet* this evening" (p. 36). Soon, in an echo of his description of the Tory government, he begins to mutter to himself that "He does it to annoy me. He knows, he *knows* I'd been looking forward to it all week" (p. 36). Preoccupied with the futile attempt to make up for lost time, Jones is anesthetized against the coming of the crisis until it is too late.

These jolts of social reality are intrusive precisely because they interrupt Jones's reveries. He keeps going off walking in parks, basking in the sun, or surrounding himself with women members of his staff who cook for him his favorite comfort foods (scrambled eggs with cream, maybe even with chili peppers). He acts as if he has plenty of time and seems unsure about whether he really wants to run in the final race. Early in the play, for instance, he is, as usual, keeping people waiting because he has disappeared in an effort to take time out from the daily round of meetings and appointments. He goes in to the park, where, he later reports, he saw people "kissing. And talking. I thought, you lucky people ... You're free, and I'm not" (p. 9). Clearly he is longing for loving contact with a woman and for relief from the pressures of time; so he basks in the sunlight in the park while others are kept waiting and while the day of political reckoning draws closer. In the end, as we have seen, he traces these longings, his uncertainty about the world and himself, and his inability to face major tests to having missed the moment of his mother's death.

There are such moments, so painful or significant that they seem to be lifted out of the ordinary flux of time. Indeed, religious experience is often centered in moments that seem to alter one's past and one's future—one's very identity in time. In the light of such moments, the past has changed or lost its meaning; and nothing in the future will ever be the same. When the momentous is enshrined in liturgy or doctrine, the individual can go through the motions of finality. In the case of Jones, that moment had never been consummated, as it were: never placed in public memory, where it could be honored and completed. Unlike the day of national mourning for those who had died in the wars of this century, with which the play began, the moment when Jones learned as a child of his mother's death was never enshrined; it seemed to go on and on.

In modern societies, I am suggesting, it is increasingly difficult for institutions to solemnize such moments; these highly important personal occasions are too numerous, too scattered, too accidental or unnoticed, and too contingent on particular circumstances to be widely shared, understood, or deeply experienced by others. Not only are individuals therefore burdened with a private grief that is difficult to share or transcend; they experience the passage of time, the loss of others, and their own temporality without the anesthetic formerly provided by a community and institutions that claim to transcend time itself.

In societies where institutions themselves are clearly provisional and therefore likely to change or disappear in time, it is difficult for a people to imagine a collective future that encompasses everyone. There is no single vision of the future, no common fate, and, hence, no shared sense of mission or destiny that gives every death a public meaning. The death of soldiers in battle is easily ascribed to the lies of the older generation, and their memory is soon lost to the generation that follows. The Vietnam War Memorial is significant to those who survive and remember, but it lacks a text to give meaning to those names for another generation that did not know the dead and cannot remember the war itself. As old grief is forgotten rather than assuaged, the future presents the prospect of continuous loss, without finality.

Secularization destroys the timeless order embodied in the state, in churches, or in communal groups that trace their history back in time over the generations and centuries. As the state's claims to transcendence come to be regarded as questionable, its charisma appears to be false: an artificial halo gilded by time, burnished by scholars who reinterpret the founding documents according to special interests and pragmatic considerations.

As the railroad and the clock have become more widespread, and as the obligation to save time and make the best use of it has become obligatory not only in industry but in everyday life, "The critique of squandered time grew and gradually separated itself from the boundaries of individual lifetimes ... the right points in time then no longer followed from nature but from the problems of synchronization, from the logistics of time itself" (Luhamnn 1995:187).

Consequently, the lifetimes of individuals come and go at a tempo that has little to do with the time span that makes sense to corporations and government agencies. It is difficult to know how far ahead a corporation may be looking: the next quarterly report or annual meeting, perhaps, or even the next turn of the business cycle. However, individuals are looking a long way down the road, not simply to the next weekend or vacation but to retirement, to death, and to the next generation. The temporal horizons of the individual may be much longer than those of an agency or corporation, if only because his or her life span may be so much shorter. Those who are running out of time often make up for this scarcity by taking a long view of their temporal horizons.

I am not suggesting that corporate executives remember only the quarterly performance of the previous year or that governmental bureaucrats remember only prior directives and not previous administrations. It is difficult to know how far back in the past a government agency may look for guidance in the present; officials may look for a statute or a legal precedent, or for a secret long buried in the archives that suddenly has relevance to a current scandal or inquiry. However, individuals may be feeling the weight of the last war or depression; they may be carrying the burden of an ancient cross or of earlier exile and exodus. The times of the individual are thus weighted with a past and open to a future that are beyond the ken and imagination of those who have the power to make the difference between life and death.

There is something cancerous about all this internal growth of organizational complexity within the nation. Anyone who has struggled to understand how and why one's HMO has decided to withhold funding for a course of treatment prescribed by one's doctor, however, knows something of what an alien feels when confronted with a bewildering set of regulations and procedures for acquiring a permit to work. The growth of organizational complexity makes the world inside the nation as if it were the outside "environment" (see Luhmann 1995:189–190). As the dissolution of the society progresses, there is less and less advantage to being on the inside.

Secularization thus cuts the individual, qua person, loose from his or her institutional moorings and exposes him or her to the loss of a world that transcends time. As individuals become free from old contexts, they increasingly make decisions not on the basis of their memberships, age, or ethnicity, but on the basis of their interests, opportunities, rights, and so forth. Abstracted from the constraints of these older categories and contexts, individuals also lack their former support and need the protection of laws based on putative rights.

Of course, the process of secularization does not occur evenly. There are always important differences between societies; within any particular society also not everyone experiences secularization in the same way or with the same force. There is ample evidence, for instance, that workers in England have long known themselves to be outside any lasting relationship to their employers; even in the fifteenth and sixteenth centuries, farmworkers knew that their tenure depended on their ability to produce.[5] The benefits and limitations of feudalism persisted even longer on the Continent than in England. There is also ample evidence that these differences have persisted into the last few decades: German workers understand their time to belong to their employers in a way that never occurred to workers in England.[6]

In the so-called nuclear family, time has been running out on the parents from the very beginning. Not only is it a matter of some urgency to enable children to support themselves; it is also incumbent upon the parents to provide for their own old age in the few years that lie between their children's departure from home and their own inevitably declining fortunes. Some have argued, in fact, that the temporal urgency of the family to secure its own and its children's future provided the drive behind the industrial revolution.[7]

Adults, therefore, experience acute time pressures in the very family that may be romanticized as being able to transcend the passage of time. Andrew Delbanco (1995:195) makes the same point very nicely when he draws on Lionel Trilling's description of "whitewashed houses in which the middle class huddled, shutting out even the sound of the crickets in which they feared to hear the 'ceaseless noise of time rushing away.'" The description comes from Trilling's novel *The Middle of the Journey*, published in 1947 at the beginnings of the rush to suburbia and the attempt to create a social world split off from the reminders of death in the cities and during the war that had just ended.

Secularity is inherently unromantic about the family and time. The secular person accepts the loss of a common framework that binds private loss to an ultimate and collective destiny. To experience secularity is to understand and accept the flow of time as linear and irreversible: to live in the full awareness that it is too late to make up for the loss of those who have died, so to speak, for us. So to live that the dead will not have died in vain is an attempt to redeem that loss by giving it meaning: not a wrong endeavor, but a hopeless one if it carries a common illusion that the living can make up for lost time. To achieve secularity, then, is to live fully exposed to the passage of time and to irredeemable loss, without the benefit of collective illusion.

The secular, then, is a way of life outside the protection of social institutions that no longer can administer grace to the living and the dead in return for various forms of obedience and tribute. The plays of David Hare are inevitably about the existential concerns of individuals whose families and social institutions seem far too temporary to act as "holding environments." For instance, as I will show in the final chapter, the heroine of *The Secret Rapture* (1988) needs more time to mourn her father. However, her family wants to speed up the process precisely so they can go about the business of making money. Indeed, it is the heroine's sister and brother-in-law who propel her into changing her studio into a modern corporation, a change that seems to the heroine intrusive and premature. Whereas the heroine wishes more time to think about life and death, the perspective of her family and their business is anything but existential; it is fiscal and corporate to a Thatcherian extreme. Someone is going to die; the love affair is coming to an end; the leader of the party will inevitably lose, even though he goes out in a final burst of activity and rhetoric. The audience mourns in advance, as it were, over the inevitable loss.

FOUR

Waiting

INCREASED EXPOSURE TO THE passage of time typifies a world that has undergone high levels of secularization. What distinguishes modernity is that individuals have lost a collective time frame that relieves their own sense of temporal anxiety. However, they continue to be caught up in an experience of time over a long span that encompasses death in both the past and the future. The individual's personal sense of time is therefore likely to be longer, more encompassing of past and future, and hence more serious than the time frames of corporations and institutions that are dealing only in relatively short-term time horizons. The modern hero is one who seizes the moment and exposes himself or herself like Faust to the "torrents of time." It is the fool who is willing to be kept waiting.

The secularization of time has made waiting exceedingly problematical. Typically to wait is the plight of the patient or subordinate, of the relatively young and helpless. Leon Altman (1957:509–10) argues that "the waiting syndrome" allows the adult to behave like a child: to believe that "time heals all things" and to adjust time "according to one's own reckoning." Those who turn waiting into a way of life, therefore, miss many opportunities and fail to mature, thus ensuring that they will be "late bloomers," if indeed they ever flourish at all. No wonder, then, that Freud preferred the injunction *carpe diem;* it is an antidote to the rebellion against time and to the tendency to be late over an entire lifetime.

However, waiting is also the inevitable plight of the individual who is forced to follow a schedule imposed by others. Waiting is the stigma of the less powerful or socially significant, of the institutionalized and the immature. Those who wait find themselves in the same company: mutual strangers with little in common beyond the circumstance of needing the same doctor or bureaucrat, mechanic or minister. The waiting room becomes a secular purgatory imposed on those whose fate depends on the schedules of professionals and bureaucrats. In modern societies those who wait may also, however, be the covert rebels who, as Altman suggested, are refusing to acknowledge the passage and limits of time. The experience of waiting, then, is full of ambiguity, ambivalence, and tension.

In the course of a long wait, one can be prey to all the parts of the self that are moribund. In the movie *As Good as It Gets,* which is indeed all about waiting, a voice near the beginning intones that "Waiting gives the devil time." The announcement has the quality of a homely bromide, like "Hope deferred makes the heart sick," and, in fact, there is little difference between waiting and "hope deferred." But it is far easier to recognize waiting as a danger to the soul when it is Satan who, in the words of an early poem from the Massachusetts Bay Colony, "lurkes amongs yow, Cunningly hee waites."[1]

There are very human limits to how long one can wait to see certain desires fulfilled. In *As Good as It Gets*, Jack Nicholson venomously plays the leading male character: an obsessive, workaholic author who literally has no time for women or children, but who is in love with a woman who waits on him—literally—at a local restaurant. His own repressions have caused him to wait far too long both for love and for therapy, and he is impatient with other patients who seem quite willing to wait for their turn with the therapist. The title of the movie comes from Nicholson's caustic question to patients in the therapist's waiting room: "Is this as good as it gets?" The answer of the movie, of course, is "No," as Nicholson learns not to keep himself waiting, or the young waitress whom he loves. In the end, they walk together into a bakery at 4:00 in the morning, the moment it opens.

If the one who waits, then, is the modern fool, there is also something disturbing, even devilish, about one who waits or keeps others waiting. The heroine of Hare's play *Skylight* (1995) arrives as a waitress, befriends the owners, and takes over the restaurant all in the same night, as she waits for the owners' return. Eventually she falls in love with the male owner of the restaurant and has an affair with him, but she inevitably leaves him the moment that the affair finally is discovered. For over a year she keeps him waiting for word from her, but in the end it is too late for them to recover their love for each other; waiting has become a way of life.

It is a strange providence that creates human beings with desires that they cannot satisfy and then makes them responsible for their failings. Hare's *Skylight* ends on the note of a secular providence; the son of the restaurant owner provides a fancy hotel breakfast for his father's ex-mistress; there is a communion of sorts between those who must wait and end up by providing for themselves. Judgment is suspended, moreover, even on the father, who was enjoying his mistress, the waitress and family friend, while his wife lay dying of cancer. The only judgment he felt was his wife's, which remained all the more censorious and haunting for having been unspoken.

Belief in providence is an acquired taste, I would argue; it does not fit those who cannot afford to wait for satisfaction. Indeed, those who have a passion for justice are typically unwilling to wait, and their passion can become "a rush to judgment." In describing eighteenth-century America, for instance, Delbanco notes that it was the more educated sectors of the population who were abandoning traditional explanations of wrongdoing such as original sin; instead, they were coming to understand the troubles of the soul as problems of the mind, and they understood the mind as a function of the brain. Thus, hallucinations and fantasies could account for errant behavior and cruel acts, and one did not need to invoke the providence of a God who created human beings with desires that they should not satisfy and who made them responsible for failings that they did not cause and could not control (Delbanco 1995:80–81).

In contrast with those who preferred rational explanations to theological arguments, Delbanco notes, were large elements of the population who still wished to see judgments made and justice done. As Jonathan Edwards put it, "The common people don't ascend up in their reflections and abstractions, to the metaphysical sources, relations, and dependences of things, in order to form their notion of faultiness or blameworthiness. They don't wait until they have decided by their refinings, what first determines the will."[2] In the absence of a belief in an overarching providence that controls history and pursues justice victoriously in the end, it is not surprising that "the common people" have trouble waiting; they can cope with only so much frustration, ambiguity, and delay. No wonder that Delbanco finds Americans in the latter part of the twentieth century caught up in the tendency to claim that they have been victimized. Instead of the war of all against all, he finds a tendency of all to fix blame broadly on others and to rush to their own judgments.

It is easy to forget what it was like to wait under highly controlled conditions, that is, under the auspices of a sacred providence. Liturgies could prescribe intense periods of waiting, in which existential anxiety could be experienced without anesthetics, precisely because the ritual guaranteed that at the decisive moment the waiting would be over and one's worst anxieties would prove to have been groundless after all. Now, however, waiting may still be somewhat ritualized, but the formalities are open-ended; one's period of waiting may be as long and as fruitless as that of Joseph K., Kafka's character who waits in vain for his case to be judged, only to be taken out at the end to die.

During the centuries in which the Church monopolized the means of grace and imposed its own system of penances, it mediated a divine providence that could impose a long wait either for forgiveness or justice. Indeed, one had to wait a stipulated time to receive benediction and grace or to have one's sins expunged through penance and remorse. As I mentioned (apropos of Gauchet's argument) in the preceding chapter, however, the Church is constantly embarrassed by a Gospel that knows no other mediation than the one provided by Christ himself in his own time and place; that "scandal of particularity" then undermines the Church's franchise on providence. Thus the Reformation broke the Church's claim that it alone could be the mediating link between heaven and earth, between divine providence and human need. Luther and others recovered the individual's own pathway to grace and claimed a foundation for the soul through faith—well outside the Church's imposition of times and places where the penitent could be kept waiting. "This day" one could be in paradise with the Lord through faith.

Thus, the Church's attempt to create a sacred universe in which the visible and invisible, the divine and the human, could be held together was destined to be torn apart by its own internal contradiction. That contradiction was part of the official dogma of the Incarnation, that God had become fully human without compromising either divinity or humanity. In the end the contradiction would make it all the more painfully obvious that such a union was beyond the capacity of ordinary mortals; it was an event once and for all despite the Church's every attempt to repeat or perpetuate it in the sacraments. As Gauchet (1976:135) puts it: "The explosive paradox of spiritual subjugation is that it legitimates a direct appeal by believers, over the system's head and over its administrators, to the ultimate source of all justice and reason. The bureaucracy of belief could not work without tacitly recognizing the autonomy of conscience." People will wait only so long for existential guarantees. Even when the Church claims a monopoly on the right to dispense certainties about the foundation of the soul and to impose waiting periods for the reception of divine assurance, the conditions have been set for an appeal "over the system's head." *The secular world has thus been created as the gospel has been progressively liberated from the Church.*

In the light of the Reformation it is easier to assert that the Church's monopoly on sacred time could not succeed indefinitely in requiring souls to wait and to be patient. In the next chapter I will describe in more detail how ritual succeeds in keeping individuals in the posture of deferential waiting. Some rituals seem able to subordinate the individual's own sense of time to that of the community with relatively little rebellion, except for the occasional outbreak of violence. It would be easy to forget how successful a religious institution may be in keeping people waiting. To forget the past would make it even more difficult, therefore, to understand why secularization has made waiting become so problematical.

The Western religious tradition is also ambiguous and ambivalent on the subject of time; witness its contradictory instructions about patience and waiting. On the one hand, the Bible is filled with reminders to tarry on the will of God. Waiting is an act of devotion, a sign of faithful patience as the believer waits for redemption or deliverance. On the other hand, the Bible is also full of injunctions to make the most of the time and to be prepared for an immediate response to human need and the divine call. On this view, waiting is merely a form of faithless passivity, a sign that the individual was unprepared to respond in a timely fashion to opportunity or danger. It is not surprising that a book filled with religious documents from a wide range of times and places, conditions, and dangers should have such diverse and inconsistent notions about waiting and about time itself. However, that diversity has placed a faithful people in historic dilemmas as they try to make sense of their past and to gain guidance for the present.

Take, as an example of biblical ambivalence toward time, the tension between active and passive messianism in Jewish tradition. "As the exile was divine punishment, only God could terminate it, and so for the majority of Jews messianism had to be passive" (Friedlander and Seligman 1994:357). On the other hand, "and in marked contradiction to the above tradition, there emerged the conception of an 'active messianism' which entailed the Jews' active participation in furthering the process of salvation."[3] Even the memorials on the Mount of Remembrance in Jerusalem reveal the tension between the passive, waiting, anti-Zionistic side of Judaism and the more active side that engages in armed resistance, seeks to establish the state, and honors military heroes (Friedlander and Seligman 1994:361ff.). I will return to this point in the next chapter. Here it is enough to note that even belief in a providential God does not relieve the believer from the dilemma of deciding how long to wait and when to act.

Within the Jesus traditions there are similarly divergent views of waiting. On the one hand, we have parables and other sayings that advocate a proactive approach to time. Perhaps a celebrity (king, bridegroom) is on the way, or perhaps there is a feast to be attended. There may be a pressing need to be met or an opportunity to be seized, and so we have the parables of the importunate widow and of the stewardship of talents. Certainly there are strands of the Jesus tradition that say that time is of the essence and that one's ability to respond to the moment is a test of one's faith; thus, we have sayings enjoining one to let the dead bury the dead and to follow Jesus immediately, just as we have stories about the need to drop all other concerns in order to find the lost spoon or other treasure. Time is always running out and it is always crucial; waiting can therefore serve only a diabolical purpose by giving the devil time, and it can be at the very least a sign of lack of faith.

However, we also have stories within the Jesus tradition that indicate that in Jesus's presence there is plenty of time. In his presence there is no further need for anxious or active preparation. Take, for example, the story of Martha and Mary, in which Jesus clearly prefers Mary's recognition that his presence defines the moment and that other duties must therefore be set aside. Take, for another example, the stories about grieving and anxious relatives who accuse Jesus of coming too late to save the sick and the dying; they are told that in his presence it is never too late and that there is plenty of time. Waiting, therefore, makes a great deal of sense to those who are assured of the Son's presence. Note, for instance, Jesus's post-resurrection injunction to his disciples to return to Jerusalem and wait for the spirit. From these stories we might develop the notion that—for those who are in communion with the divine presence—there is plenty of time.

Taken together, the two strands in the traditions about Jesus provide Christianized cultures with a quite irreconcilable conflict with regard to time. Therefore, one is in something of a limbo about the relation of the present to the past or the future. On the one hand, the present is to be liberated from the past so that the future may begin, with not a moment to waste; on the other hand, the only faithful thing to do is to wait in patient hope and expectation because the divine presence has already been given. Waiting is the only way to be faithful, and action is an illusion. However, waiting may cause one to miss the chance of a lifetime.

It is possible that this cultural ambivalence about waiting reflects—and may stem from—the dilemmas of everyday life. On the one hand, when someone delays a response, waiting may be ominous:

> Being kept waiting is an insult because it unilaterally delays the kind of "quality encounter" that one has mentally and physically organized one's life around. We are irritated at those who take outside calls, gaze out the window, or read newspapers during *our* interaction with them. Such inattentiveness implies not just that the other person is "busy" but spills over and indicates something about the substance of the conversation: that it is not taken as very

important or that the answer to a request will be no. (Boden and Molotch 1994: 264)

On the other hand, waiting may be disappointing but benign. The same authors, a few pages later, acknowledge that being kept waiting may be a token of the other's intention to let one down slowly, a kind attitude that promises better things in the future:

> When people delay a negative response to allow withdrawal of a request, they have taken it on themselves to protect the other interactant—and they have done so without there being any explicit rule, norm, or law requiring them to do so. This consideration implies to the requester that subsequent interactions with the responder will likewise be benign, perhaps then coloring the *substance* of what goes on as the interactants make assumptions about one another's intentions in regard to honoring promises, pacts, and contracts." (Boden and Molotch 1994: 267)

To give meaning to these signs from a religious vantage point may or may not work since the true significance of delay can only be known in the outcome. However, the outcome depends on how one reads and responds to certain signs in the meantime. All one can do is buy time by delaying an immediate and unreflective response; indeed, it takes time to try to decipher what is contained between the lines of a message and to read all the other signs that are available in order to know how best to respond. No wonder that intelligence gathering is a major preoccupation of modern corporations, just as deception and spying are chronic themes of mass entertainment. Nothing is just what it seems, and waiting may even be necessary in order to avoid a premature and disastrous reaction. Conversely, the necessity to wait may in itself mean that one's fate is in the hands of others who are anything but benign.

Waiting in quiet helplessness opens up the vista of an indefinite stretch of time that may end in nothing: a glimpse of an abyss within the self that seems foreign, strange, uncanny, and therefore threatening. Indeed, Delbanco (1995: 43) notes that for the New Englander the devil "was not an outsider; he was invasive, internal." Sometimes that internal space is imagined to be full of invisible and potent forces. For the Puritans, the community—not the wilderness and the

Indians—was the place that harbored the devil, and the community could be torn apart by self-righteousness and greed. For many of the first New Englanders, the notion of evil was abstract, if only because the world in which they lived was increasingly complex and filled with a variety of opportunities and terrors that were difficult to name (Delbanco 1995: 44). If it was difficult to personify and place evil outside the settlement, the devil must be lying in wait within the community and the church. By the same reasoning, the dwelling place of evil was within the soul, which could harbor the worst of passions while maintaining an outward show of conformity and piety (Delbanco 1995: 45).

Waiting may bring out the worst in the individual: a hope that one be spared the deadly implications of being kept waiting, while others, if necessary, will suffer them. As Delbanco (1995: 229–30) puts it, "The potentiality to seek life through the dehumanization of others lurks within all persons and all cultures—a fact that the great American writers, working within the Augustinian tradition, have tried to resist by exposing it." Thus, we have a cultural tradition and a sacred institution that create two rather acutely different forms of waiting. One aspect of the cultural tradition dignifies waiting as a duty; the other finds waiting either spiritually dangerous or a great impediment to spiritual progress. Chronic waiting, therefore, may be not only self-defeating but quite cruel in its impact on others, an ambiguity that comes alive in the plays of David Hare. Remember Jones, the impatient and yet unprepared Labour Party candidate in *The Absence of War*, who managed to keep others waiting and to defeat himself as well.

The problem is twofold: a missing providence that has dissolved into contrary maxims about time in general and about waiting in particular, and a complex society that has little regard for the individual per se. Whether or not one is advised to wait or to seize the day, the cultural injunctions are at best confusing, and there is no overarching assurance that in God's own good time the contradictions will be resolved. To this cultural injury, so to speak, is added the insult to the narcissism of the individual who finds little in the way of the self and its needs mirrored in the routines and agendas of most corporations and institutions. On the one hand, individuals are required to subordinate their needs and agendas to the schedule and calendar of organizations and elites; personal needs are held in abeyance so that as client or employee one can be on time. However, modern societies also put a premium on time, and individuals who engage in an imaginary fantasy world are regarded not as pious or visionary but as developmentally arrested: psychological rebels against the passage of time.

The contemporary theater offers us an interesting example of the tension between various attitudes toward waiting. In *Racing Demon,* Hare dramatizes the tension between two ways in which religion has orchestrated the problem of waiting. One of the main characters is Lionel, the senior clergyman of a parish in South London situated in a relatively poor and working-class parish, although still frequented by some members of the middle class with Thatcherite tendencies. Lionel is busy: he hands out schedules to other members of the parish clergy, prefers not to use religious language when ordinary speech will do, labors hard over his sermons, and largely ignores his wife, whose health has been slowly declining and who appears on the verge of collapse. Although obsessive about agendas, schedules, and deadlines, he seems remarkably unconcerned by the fact that he is running out of time in his marriage, as well as in his position as rector of this parish. In a conversation with a much younger woman, Frances, Lionel learns that she sees him as a man like her father, who was also a dreamer and who wasted time—indeed wasted his life—in religious fantasy. Clearly Lionel hides anxieties about the passage of time under a mask of professional activity, using a life of service to others as a cover for keeping them waiting.

The sadistic and self-destructive aspects of the rebellion against time are thus easy to observe in one who is a virtuoso at waiting. Lionel is the picture of patience and forbearance; however, he has kept his family and the people of his parish waiting for so long that signs of impatience are all around him. Thus, Lionel's time has begun to run out. The bishop of Southwark wants him removed so that he can be replaced with a cleric who is strong, optimistic, and full of the Gospel. Time has run out for Lionel in other ways as well. His marriage has long since been defunct, and his wife is showing signs of disintegration after suffering a stroke toward the end of the play. Worried for his wife, Lionel once again calls upon Frances for company; not quite incidentally, she is also the former lover of Lionel's junior clergyman, Tony. To Frances Lionel makes a strange confession. It seems that Lionel's wife, long seen to be ailing, has finally had a stroke and for a long time had lain undiscovered on the kitchen floor. After calling an ambulance for help, however, Lionel had had to tell the drivers that he did not know how long it was that his wife had been lying on the floor. His inadvertence was due to the fact that he had been preparing a sermon on the poll tax in another room and had been trying to "get it right" (Hare 1991: 57). Not only does Lionel keep others waiting while he pays his debts to schedules and deadlines but he manages also to be late for each successive, critical test.

Criticized for being perfunctory in his liturgical performances, Lionel is a man clearly preoccupied with other times and places, seldom fully present and often, therefore, personally ineffective. Lionel is strangely disconnected from the passage of time in his own life, and he watches with apparent disengagement as his marriage and his ministry slowly fall apart, as if he could somehow transcend the passage of time.

It would appear that Lionel's tendency to wait life out while others languish is due to his own absorption elsewhere; it is a strategy for appearing to be on time while he busies himself with schedules, while in fact he is transported to another realm in which time does not run out. Thus, in a chess game with Frances Lionel makes a number of inattentive and self-defeating moves. Not surprisingly, she is prompted to ask him if he is suicidal or has a death wish, to which he answers quite simply, "Yes. I'm sorry" (p. 58). It is left to Frances to say what must be said to Lionel when he explains that both his children have left home quite angry and that he is totally out of touch with one of them, his daughter Lucy:

LIONEL: I must say, it is odd. I know so many clergy families
           where the children have gone. They seem to get very
           angry. Was it like that for you?

FRANCES: A bit. My father's only a layman. I mean, of course I
           was angry for a while.

LIONEL: Yes. Why is that?

(She pauses for a moment.)

FRANCES: Because it all seems such a waste.

LIONEL: What kind of a waste?

FRANCES: Of a human being. To have his mind all the time on something else. Always to be dreaming.

LIONEL: Is that how it seems?

FRANCES: Well, yes, it does. (p. 58)

Lionel's tendency to turn waiting into a way of life is expressed in his dreaming. He is enchanted by Frances and is reluctant to let her go, even though there is no possibility of an affair between them. His compromise is to hang on to her in a world of fantasy. Frances, indeed, reminds him that he is dreaming, and he admits it in the end. Frances also has to remind him that he should be with his very sick and despairing wife, who represents the very running out of time that Lionel has been refusing to face.

Lionel is thus a mixture of interesting contradictions. On the one hand, he sees himself as authentic, but he is perceived by Frances and others to be a bit unreal and dreamy. Seeking to give others immediate access to the Church, he keeps them waiting for more tangible or practical forms of help. Unwilling to raise barriers to membership, since the Church and the faith are for all, he finds membership in his congregation dwindling. For Lionel Christian faith is about providing an anchorage for identity through participation in the Church's worship and through membership in the Christian community; thus, the Church must not allow religious language to get in the way of faith:

> The moment you start using all the language, you distance people. And it's not important. He's there. He loves people whether they know it or not. Why put them off with all the cultural baggage? It sets up a resistance. They're bored before you even get into all that stuff . . . So much of what passes for religion is simply nonsense. Close the church doors and all tell God how wonderful he is. Where does that get you? And the more people doing it, the more you're said to be thriving. It's phoney." (pp. 59–60)

Despite his high regard for immediate access to the circle of faith, Lionel has kept everyone waiting for too long. That is perhaps why his wife, Heather, calls Lionel the "foolish virgin," in a clear reference to the parable of the wise and foolish virgins in the New Testament (p. 28). The virgins were foolish, of course, because they did not recognize that the time was coming for the Bridegroom to draw near, and so their lamps were not filled with oil. Just as Frances has caught Lionel dreaming, Heather has unmasked the hidden identity of a boy confused in his own mind with a virgin mother. The wife's diagnosis is shared by the bishop. Indeed, Lionel's passivity has offended the bishop:

> You're a joke, Lionel. You stand in the centre of the parish like some great fat wobbly girl's blouse. Crying for humanity. And doing absolutely nothing at all. . . . Yes, I chose you. Because you are the reason the whole church is dying. Immobile. Wracked. Turned inward. Caught in a cycle of decline. Your personal integrity your only concern. Incapable of reaching out. A great vacillating pea-green half-set jelly . . . It truly offends me, the idea that people need authority, and every time they come to ask what does the church think then they are hit in the face by a spurt of lukewarm water from a rugby bladder. And I simply will not allow it to go on . . . There's something in your tone which is sanctimonious. You give an appearance of superiority which is wholly unearned . . . It's profoundly offensive. Because it is based on nothing at all. You parade your so called humility, until it becomes a disgusting kind of pride. Yes, we can all be right if we never actually *do* anything. (pp. 79–80)

It may seem unfair of the bishop to attack so busy a man as Lionel for not doing anything, but the playwright here is revealing the illusion of action as perhaps the worst sin of all. Beneath the cloak of activity is concealed someone who is simply waiting in a dreamlike state of suspended animation, as if he had all the time in the world. Those who are in secret possession of a rapture all their own of course do not need to hasten the day of redemption.

If Lionel seemed eager to allow people immediate access to the life of the Church without keeping them waiting, he himself seemed to have all the time in the world; no wonder he could wait indefinitely. Although he despised phoniness in religion, his wife and his bishop see him as a fake: "sanctimonious," a virgin posing as a man, a "wobbly girl" disguised as a loving and devoted priest. Beneath Lionel's busy-ness we find a fantasy of tranquil fusion with the source of life, but the fantasy is self-destructive. As Frances observed at the chess-board, Lionel is not only a dreamer with time to spare; he is also someone with a suicidal streak that wishes to see an end to his long waiting and suffering. Asked why he thinks that the bishop chose to make an example of him, Lionel says, "Because he thought I would go" (Hare 1991: 81).

Lionel, as we have seen, is biding his time, keeping others waiting, preparing for a confrontation with patriarchal authority, and in the meantime enjoying in a dreamy fashion a quiet satisfaction. Finally, however, liberated by the bishop's rejection, Lionel stands his ground. In fact, he has consulted a lawyer who assures him that he would have legal grounds for fighting his dismissal, and the local clerical union is eager to take on his case as a means of recruiting among the clergy. It is as if he needed the wake-up call from the bishop in order to recognize that his time was nearly over.

There are some who would want a good bit more than that un-mediated access. When a Jamaican woman named Stella (as in Stella Marie, the Virgin Mary's old epithet) comes to him for help, she leaves disappointed. Stella has had an abortion, is afraid of her hus-band, and is deeply depressed. Lionel prays for her, offers her friend-ship, and lets her go. No wonder that she is baffled that there is noth-ing more to it:

STELLA: Will that help?

LIONEL: I don't know. It can't do any harm.

(*He gets up to say goodbye to her.*)

... I don't know if God'll help you. But now you do have a friend. You have me. This house is always open. Whenever you're lonely.

STELLA: Oh, I see. Is that it?

LIONEL: Yes. (*Nods*). That is the service.

STELLA: Oh. (*Stands a moment, uncertain.*) Well, thanks very much.

*(He smiles at her as she leaves. Then turns his attention to
the piles of duplicated papers on the table.)*

LIONEL: Tony, hello, I apologize, *the clock overtook me."* (pp.
11–12; emphasis added)

Note that when Tony, a junior cleric on the staff, enters Lionel's office, Lionel has a sudden reminder of time (the clock that "overtook"
him) and busies himself again with his papers. In this momentary
time-out with Stella, there is instant access, with no questions asked,
nothing phony, and a guarantee of membership in the house of God
as a friend of Lionel. Nothing more. In an order that does not question one's identity or membership but confers upon one immediate
friendship without question, there is apparently no waiting, no requirements for admission. It is a timeless order, based on eternal access to the throne of grace. In a timeless social order, there is only the
givenness of things either to accept or reject. One does not have to
worry or wonder about how things could have been otherwise, since
all the contingencies have been eliminated. The intrusion of time,
like Tony's entrance, is always something of a surprise: the clock, as
it were, gets ahead of one because one has been wasting time in a fantasy of transcendence. Lionel, therefore, does not trouble himself
with alternative courses of action, but Tony is very much concerned
with what has not been considered or attempted in the case of that
desperate and depressed woman from Jamaica, Stella Marie. Tony
wants to know "what will happen to her?" but Lionel simply says
"I don't know" and turning "hopelessly" discusses the failure of the
doctors and the social services to be of any use. As for Tony's suggestion that Lionel tell her "about Christ," Lionel objects that he
does not like to use others' sorrows as an occasion for Christian
salesmanship, a clear slap at Tony, who before being ordained had
been a beer salesman. Undaunted, Tony suggests the need for a
"team policy" to deal with a case like Stella's, but Lionel counters that
she is not a case but a "person." As to whether she will develop a
religious "dimension" that will make her life "easier," Lionel is
comfortably agnostic—"on the other hand, maybe she won't"—an
acceptance than shocks the younger, more evangelical clergyman
(pp. 12–13).

Lionel is superficially secular, and he appears to draw the line between the possible and the impossible. There is little he can do, and there is no point in referring Stella to doctors and social workers who will simply refer her, in the long run, back to him. However, beneath this secular and pragmatic surface, he is quite unrealistic about time and enjoys a world of private fantasy. In those interior recesses of his psyche, Lionel tends to be oblivious to the passage of time and the loss of opportunity. No wonder Lionel believes that he can afford to wait. Tony, on the other hand, is apparently living in an enchanted world; because he has sustained unbearable losses, his grasp of reality is never entirely firm. It is not surprising that Tony's world is therefore full of untold possibility, as well as of untold agony. His perception of limits is rather vague, and the impossible may indeed seem possible at any and every moment. With Tony and God, all things are possible all the time. Beneath this enchantment, however, lies an experience of unbearable and final loss.

However, Hare has his own tendency to rebel against time. Hare considers his characters as imperfect, but they are to be purified through the passage of time. Thus, it is necessary for them to wait, if only because they are, as Hare notes in his introduction to *The History Plays* (1984), "impure" reflections of various "ideas and ideals." Hare (1984: 13) confesses that he has been criticized for bringing the story of his characters prematurely "up to date," and "given the chance again, I would stomp through the years with less heavy boots." Evidently it is hard for the playwright to wait to see his characters come to fruition, but waiting is necessary if only because it takes time for his audiences to come to terms with the plays. They may prefer a "simpler morality" to the one that seems to govern the fate of his characters (p. 13). Even though time does seem to be on the side of the playwright, it is difficult for Hare to wait until critics and audiences understand his characters properly. Speaking of the purification of his plays from previous recriminations, he writes: "For some reason it seems to take my audiences and my critics time to allow this process. *Of course I wish it were otherwise*."[4]

Waiting is at its most suspenseful during the convergence of disparate worlds. In Hare's *Racing Demon,* it is the Jamaican woman and the Anglican cleric, the church and the community, the abstracted husband and the dying wife, the evangelist and the hungry world whose convergence makes waiting problematic and intense. In antiquity, the heralded arrival of Caesar's representatives to cities, whether to grant tax benefits or to announce new austerities, initiated a period of dramatic anticipation and enforced waiting. Such imperative suspense is echoed in the sayings attributed to Jesus about a Bridegroom who comes and must find his party prepared to receive him or about a distant landholder who finally arrives to receive a full accounting of his stewards' performance in his absence.[5] Even without such dramatized convergences, however, the center impinges on the periphery at certain times of the year: for example, at the deadline for filing taxes. At such times the center issues reminders not to wait, not to delay or postpone, that allow the center to be seen as fateful, possessed of the grace to extend a deadline.

It is not only in the convergence of the center on the periphery that waiting becomes obligatory. Waiting is required whenever those of differing social status come together. Waiting is inherent in the asymmetrical relationship between those who have information or skills and the people who, as clients or patients, need them. No wonder, then, that as the center converges on the periphery or as those in need attend those who are in a position to provide various benefits, ceremony enjoins postures of deference and waiting. What is deferred is the individuals' ability to dispose of their own time and fate.

FIVE

Ritual and the Consummation of Waiting

LIVING AS WE DO IN THE residues of the Reformation, it is easy for us to forget how successfully the Church once was able to bureaucratize the time of salvation and to keep people waiting as though their very souls depended on the Church's dispensation from the passage of time. In some locales, of course, that old ecclesiastical monopoly persists. Take, for example, the ritual called Sabta Nur performed annually at the Church of the Holy Sepulchre in Jerusalem. According to the description given by Richard Hecht (1994: 184–235), members of various competing ethnic groups suspend their rivalry on these occasions as they crowd into the church to wait for the gift of holy fire to descend. The divine gift is given annually, right on time, to the archbishops of the Greek and Armenian Orthodox communities who are at the critical moment concealed behind doors in the innermost chamber of the church. The archbishops are buried, as it were, alive in this tomb, and their symbolic death is reflected in the suspension of all animation among the worshipers who wait with intense anxiety outside the doors for the fire once more to descend and then to be transmitted to the expectant worshipers from each of the rival communities.

Although the gift has never failed, in the moments while people are waiting for the fire to appear, there is heavy silence, punctured by anguished beatings of the chest and moans of agonized anticipation.

The question is whether the real presence of God will appear, and the longing for that presence is palpable, audible, tangible as people wait, once again, for the final reassurance that they are not alone. Just before receiving the fire, men and women display terrible anxiety that the fire will be withheld and they will be disappointed. Never mind that the fire has arrived precisely on time for several centuries; it is the ritual's work to heighten the anxiety of waiting in order that relief should be all the more palpable.

Between the ethnic groups crowded into the compact and enclosed space of the interior of the church itself, there is still a great social distance, but the ritual as a whole honors each group in its proper physical and social location. By arrangements made under the Ottomans in the nineteenth century, each ethnic and religious group has its assigned place in the service, carefully marked out by chalk lines and barriers. Similarly, the way that the holy fire is received and distributed keeps Greeks and Armenians on relatively equal terms; other ethnic groups receive a clearly lesser status by having to wait moments longer to receive the holy fire. When the pilgrims light their candles from the sacred fire, a renewed community emerges from the church. The ritual is a model, therefore, of how the Christian community can give adequate narcissistic satisfaction to the members of a variety of disparate and competing groups. Each person leaves with his or her own standing in the community enlightened and affirmed.

Waiting is often enjoined when close physical or emotional proximity may give people an opportunity to hurt each other. There is something about forced association, as Erving Goffman (1961) has pointed out, that is threatening to the self; to find oneself in the company of others whose status undermines one's own is a form of symbolic invasion of the self that makes people understandably very anxious. Here the point is that a threat of violence to the individual hangs over these mysterious proceedings in which holy fire is finally allowed to erupt under carefully controlled conditions. The suspense of waiting for the fire to be given is thus intensified by the knowledge that, when members of these groups are crowded together, unholy passions may also erupt with fatal consequences. Worshipers have been known to stash weapons in the church in preparation for sudden battle, and in the nineteenth century indeed there were stampedes in which worshipers were trampled to death. One waits, therefore, not only in longing but in fearful anticipation of death itself: a controlled experiment, as it were, in existential anxiety.

The rite is all the more effective because few are concentrating on the fact that their relative social standing has depended on the edicts of a dead empire. It is the Ottomans whose rules for this limited engagement are still in force, long after their empire has disappeared. The rules were made necessary because the rite of holy fire occasionally ended in an unholy combustion of ethnic rivalry and outright violence; indeed Hecht (1994: 218–20) describes several occasions in the nineteenth century when many were injured and died in terrible melees. That is why it became necessary for the Ottomans to legislate the rules that have henceforth come to be known as the Status Quo. It is not only to keep waiting from being unbearable but satisfaction from being revolutionary that ritual so carefully calibrates its rewards to the faithful.

Even the most devoted of those who wait for the fire, however, may not be reflecting as they wait on how they are reinforcing ancient Ottoman authority or a Muslim lineage by taking part in this rite. The chalk lines in the floor prescribe not only a place to stand in the church but one's standing in the community. By waiting until his or her ethnic group has received the fire in proper order, one accepts a certain rank in the communal scheme of things, a rank determined by powers that are by now nameless and forgotten but all the more potent for being considered part of the necessary scheme of things. The worshipers thus have a certain false consciousness, in the Marxist meaning of the phrase; they think they are acting voluntarily even while they are acting in such a way as to reinforce the authority of the system. By failing to doubt the right of the authorities to determine one's standing in the community or to require one to wait for the essentials of life, one becomes a willing dupe of the system. Catherine Bell (1992: 108) is more kind in her discussion of the blindness of the ritualized psyche and speaks only of "a strategic misrecognition of the relationship of one's ends and means."

Earlier I suggested that ritual not only embodies a providential universe but provides ample narcissistic satisfaction to the individual, who is assured that his or her existence has been recognized and valued by the larger society or particular institution performing the rite in question. It is also true, however, that these guarantees and satisfactions come at a price: the institutionalization of waiting. Ritual promises to end a period of longing and waiting, but it also recasts anticipation on a longer temporal horizon. On the one hand, people come together from disparate worlds for a short time and share in a common universe, in which they have the experience of at least glimpsing others' worlds as though from the inside. The use of common language and the self-disclosure of various hearts in confession or song create temporary social universes with lasting effect. On the other hand, ritual embodies an element of erotic teasing that promises and partially delivers timeless satisfaction. In the end, ritual requires one to come back, later, after a period of further waiting. Although ritual promises that its enactment ends the long period of waiting, there is an element of carefully contrived mystery that perpetuates the experience of waiting—for example, until next year in Jerusalem, or until the Second Coming when all secrets will be revealed, and so on.

Waiting is turned into a way of life, moreover, when rituals lose their monopoly on social control; then everyday routines become somewhat solemnized. Through the ritualization of everyday life, people are kept waiting, and mundane ceremonies perpetuate certain mysteries in order to keep people coming back. No one knows this better than the people who wait for governmental agencies to work on their cases. Perhaps the most ordinary example of ritualized social life is the doctor's office, where disparate worlds meet but in which certain medical mysteries remain and people return to find out about their cases over long periods of time. There everyone is required to become patient. With ritualization, providential guarantees are replaced by the policy of the office in question, each office having its own procedures and each institution its own priorities. Consequently, individuals lose whatever narcissistic satisfactions they once enjoyed, especially when their identity is recognized in the most impersonal fashion, as by a number.

It may be helpful here to say what I mean by "ritualization," and for that purpose I can think of no better choice than the following passage from Bell's (1992: 74) discussion of ritual:

I will use the term "ritualization" to draw attention to the way in which social actions strategically distinguish themselves in relation to other actions. In a very preliminary sense, ritualization is a way of acting that is designed and orchestrated to distinguish and privilege what is being done in comparison to other, usually more quotidian, activities. As such, ritualization is a matter of various culturally specific strategies for setting some activities off from others, for creating and privileging a qualitative distinction between the "sacred" and the "profane," and for ascribing such distinctions to realities thought to transcend the powers of human actors.

Ritualized actions keep some people waiting on others with higher social standing. Those who attend on others must wait, be patient, even suffer; their time is not their own. Nowhere is this danger more apparent than in the places that Goffman calls "total institutions": places like asylums and prisons, concentration camps, and monasteries or convents, where one's simplest action is likely to be suspended by orders from those placed higher in the chain of local command. Of course, every schoolchild knows what it is like to have to wait to go to the bathroom until one is given permission by the teacher, and in schools waiting is often used as a punishment called "detention." To detain individuals is to make them wait and to inhibit their ability to walk and talk, to act and to speak for themselves like ordinary self-determining and self-respecting adults. That is Goffman's point regarding patients in mental institutions:

> [O]ne of the most telling ways in which one's economy of action can be disrupted is the obligation to request permission or supplies for minor activities that one can execute on one's own on the outside, such as smoking, shaving, going to the toilet, telephoning, spending money, or mailing letters. This obligation not only puts the individual in a submissive or suppliant role 'unnatural' for an adult but also opens up his line of action to interceptions by staff. *Instead of having his request immediately and automatically granted, the inmate may be teased, denied, questioned at length, not noticed, or, as an ex-mental patient suggests, merely put off:*
> "Even the canteen staff seemed to share the opinion that civility was wasted on lunatics, and would keep a patient waiting indefinitely, while they gossiped with their friends."[1]

Even the most ordinary church service requires people to wait until the minister begins the service, to bow heads or bend knees on command, to confess their faults in front of strangers, to have others see them in various postures of submission no matter how dignified or powerful they may be in everyday life, and to hold up their hands as they wait to receive a blessing or a token of spiritual food from those in authority. Although some people are obviously eager to get out of church and to reestablish themselves as self-determining adults by having a cup of coffee or a good talk among friends, others who develop a taste for being infantilized by the Church may stay on in various roles in which they wait on others just as they wait to be instructed by the clergy.

Waiting thus becomes a way of avoiding adult responsibilities at the price of being kept in a relatively infantile status by those who have the right to come and go as they please. Think for a moment of the butler in the film *Remains of the Day,* played superbly on the screen by Anthony Hopkins. For years this butler waits on his master, who is a British conservative and aristocrat with fascist tendencies and associations, a man to whom the butler sacrifices even his loyalty to his own father. As the butler's father lies dying and wishes to have a final word with his son, the butler leaves him in order to perform his duties to his master's guests, one of whom has developed a blister on his foot and needs attention. The butler returns to his father too late and finds him dead the next morning. In the same way the butler clearly has fallen in love with the housekeeper, a lovely woman played with grace and reserve by Emma Thompson, but even after being released from service to his master the butler is unable to speak of his love or ask her to marry him, and they part with unspoken longing for each other's presence and mute with pain. The butler has waited too long.

Waiting is also what one does precisely on the margins of the social world, and it is on the margins that time is always running out. Conversely, social systems have their own ways of making sure that they do not run out of time, that time is on their side, and that when decisions are made they are taken with as much deliberation and as little hurry as possible. Claus Offshe (1996:28) notes that modern institutions are pressed for time precisely because they have to cope with so much internal complexity and with so competitive an environment; he advises them that

> It would be consistent with . . . a criterion of rational decision, disciplined in the temporal dimension, if the method of taking decisions prescribed that they were not taken under the time pressure exerted by competing decision-makers, but rather were taken— for instance, through the introduction of moratoria or iterative decision procedures—with the time necessary to enable evaluation of possible subsequent effects.

Those who are marginal or who are not given the full array of adult responsibilities are the most vulnerable to narcissistic wounds in the bureaucratic or competitive institutions of a modern society. In the waiting room of the doctor's office, for instance, one is simply a temporary appointment. Like the butler in *Remains of the Day*, one has a status in the household or practice that is marginal at best, and one has ample opportunity to reflect on a life held for the time being in abeyance. Similarly, in Kafka's *The Trial,* Joseph K. waits just outside the judge's quarters, always on the threshold of being told his fate.

Those who are schooled in a highly ritualized institution, like the clergy, may be the last to understand the narcissistic injury imposed on others who are forced to wait. Time, after all, is on the side of those in positions of sufficient power to be waited upon and to keep others waiting. When those positions are sanctified by tradition or institutional authority, as in the case of the clergy, the cleric can afford to keep others in suspense. Of course, not all clerics will feel themselves equally endowed with time; the younger, those of lower status, and those haunted by their own particular forms of existential anxiety will find waiting dreadful and will identify themselves with those who experience time with a certain dread.

Ritual thus enables those in power to create an environment that they are likely to control through various symbols and gestures.[2] When that environment changes, of course, those who controlled the ritualized distribution of time may well feel rudely surprised. Remember Lionel, Hare's clerical character, whose awakenings come in the form of a dying wife, an impatient junior colleague, a woman in trouble, and, finally, an outraged bishop. Those whose ability to stand on ceremony allows them to wait and to keep others waiting are subject to rude awakenings.

In other words, rituals train people to wait for the signal to be given from above, as it were: the signal that the time has come, whether it is to fight, or to make a final sacrifice, or to join hands in reconciliation. Individuals who are less subject to ritualized controls will be more likely to shape their own environment, to be able to play with the meaning of signs and signals, to avoid passing premature judgment, to remain flexible in determining their own and others' responses, to sense the unprecedented, and to identify opportunities and threats. They may wait to make up their own minds, but they are not likely to be kept waiting by those who stand on ceremony.

Ritual trains a people to wait for authorization to act, while enduring perhaps untold existential agony. Rituals are thus a command performance in which a society trains its members not to go off half-cocked, as it were, but to wait for command or permission to be given. One is not to rush to judgment on others but to allow the deity, or his or her clerical representatives, to pass judgment. Thus, rituals are a line of defense against panic and civil war. They are also the source of a tendency to wait until commanded to act and to defer to higher authority.[3] For Luhmann (1995:185),

> Ritualizations, religious and otherwise, . . . translate external uncertainties into an internal schematism that either happens or not, but that cannot be varied, and therefore neutralizes the capacity for deception, lies, and deviant behavior. Ritualizations make little claim on the system's complexity. Therefore they appear to be helpful as long as adequately complex systems capable of developing functional equivalences to absorb uncertainty do not emerge in the form of organizations.

This is a point with obvious implications for churches that have long since discovered that they need complex forms of social organization to cope with social problems that are not cured by their liturgies. For instance, the churches have developed denominational agencies and a large-scale bureaucracy to respond to social problems ranging from AIDS and homelessness to a degraded environment and hostile religionists from other cultures. There is little left of a providential viewpoint; advisory committees tend to prefer their own most recent publications on social policy. There is also little narcissistic satisfaction for the laity in surveying the denominational offerings and agencies; the emphasis of the Church on relevant expertise suggests that the laity and even the clergy are ill equipped to deal with so much uncertainty in the larger society and the world itself.

In the meantime, people get tired of waiting for authoritative answers to their questions about what to do with their lives, whom to trust, what to believe in, and when to die. The times of the churches increasingly seem to follow the tempos of bureaucracies, and their rituals respond to the seasons of a Church year, all of which are out of synchrony with the ups and downs of everyday life and individual lifetimes.

Those who live in a period of cybernetic communication may have very little patience with a world in which one is obliged to wait out one's lifetime in ways that reinforce the authority of an ancient order and its agents. For those who engage in global communication by entering a search word on the Internet and discover literally thousands of possible sites for further investigation, it may be difficult to see any social order as being other than voluntary and emergent. While a ritualized order that enshrines the past can legitimately require one to wait indefinitely, a social order that emerges as one makes one's own tentative choices and hopes for a useful response is evanescent as well as emergent, a very chancy thing that may last only if one makes a bookmark, so to speak, to recall the site. In a cybernetic world waiting is reduced to a function of the speed of one's processor. Such a world is not conducive to the laity's waiting for the latest official pronouncement from the Church on various subjects.

In a ritualized social order one can more easily believe in a providential God whose decrees and intentions unfold over time as one waits for fresh signs of divine recognition of one's own obedience or faithlessness. In a cybernetic world, however, God is legitimately considered more of a process in which the future is determined by a series of human choices that might well not have been made. In such a world the rapid exchange of information makes ritualized waiting difficult and sometimes dangerous. Waiting becomes more continuous, more chronic, less intense, perhaps, and always filled with revised anticipation. Individuals may be caught up in such a rapid flow of events and messages that they are left to themselves, as it were, to experience the anxiety of the future and to feel the burden of their past. Waiting in an open and complex society, unlike the ritualized apprehension of the devotees in the Church of the Holy Sepulchre, becomes a more fluid and private affair, like waiting for the report from the doctor or the next dip in the financial market.

In the days immediately before the opening of the Gulf War, Operation Desert Storm, I and some of my friends experienced a form of dread: a heavy apprehension was in the air, so to speak, and we ourselves felt weighed down by time. Quite another experience of time was more recently played out in the Pentagon as the military prepared strikes in retaliation for Iraq's refusal to cooperate with the UN arms inspection team. In a Sunday edition of the *New York Times* a writer described this development in the "Theater of War: The New Face of Battle Wears Greasepaint":

> The air war between the United States and Iraq has already begun.
>
> Not the one waged with smart bombs and Tomahawk missiles, but the one fought with laptop computers and satellite transmitters. The mission: to hit hard, in real air time, with precisely targeted television images designed to have an immediate impact on policy makers, military planners, and public opinion. . . .
>
> The first time America went to war against Saddam Hussein, seven years ago, American strategists hadn't anticipated how much influence instant imagery would have on warmaking, and they were stunned.
>
> This time much more is known about broadcasting technology and how far it can reach, and the Pentagon is trying to adjust to how unpredictably an instant image of battle can skew a viewer's opinion of the war itself. So military planners have held countless sessions *to figure out how to fight a war in a media-smart way.* . . .
>
> *"You have to pay attention to how a war appears on television these days, there's no way around it,"* said Kenneth Bacon, the Pentagon spokesman. *"It's not the controlling factor in designing a mission. But it is a factor." (Sciolino 1998: 4.1; emphasis added)*

There you have it. Time is shorter for modern societies because the rate of anticipated response keeps going up. Of course, time is always running out just before a war, but in the case of current battles time is in short supply not only because military action and military response have to be calculated in advance but because the media have sped up reaction time both in Baghdad and in the United States, where the public and planners are getting more information than ever before and have a greater impact on the conduct of the war itself. That leaves individuals little time to reflect on the past and the present on their own. As the time zone of public policy becomes increasingly short and the memories of the past offer only limited guidance for the future, the future impinges on every "message" and anticipated response. The individuals who go off to war to die must cope with a longer and yet a far less elastic time frame; their memories may stretch far into the past as well as toward the prospect of death. Eternity becomes a private preoccupation that escapes the intensified give-and-take of the war room and the media.

As bombs become messages, moreover, those receiving them are becoming more sophisticated in their responses. An intuitive, "knee-jerk" response to the brilliance of the Pentagon's technology is increasingly unlikely, as the public learns that the images and their implications being broadcast from the front are increasingly calculated to shape public response. The notion of "war games" takes on new meaning as the role of politicians and the media becomes more explicit and widely known than it was, say, in the First World War. Furthermore, the public gains some reaction time by distinguishing the information sent back to them about the war from the message that the generals wish to convey. Thus, a picture intended to demonstrate American superiority on the ground and in the air may be taken by the public as a sign of America's willingness to take cruel and unnecessary advantage of an enemy in disarray and retreat. Not only will the message therefore be understood quite differently from the way the generals wished it to be taken, but it may also be rejected. Instead of instant assent and compliance, reflection on the meaning conveyed by a message offers a way of gaining a little time.

There was a time when war was more highly ritualized. For instance, in his essay "Cubism, Camouflage, Silence, and Democracy,"

Stephen Kern (1994: 163–80) notes the ritualized conduct of war even into the first months of the First World War. At the outset the French were still dressing their soldiers in the bright colors of the Second Empire, which had once served the purpose of intimidating the enemy soldiers. As a result, however, the soldiers made very good targets indeed for enemy artillery and machine guns that had a much longer range than the old musketry.

Kern goes on to point out that the ritualized aspects of modern warfare collapsed not only for practical reasons, such as the need to camouflage the troops and artillery positions, but because democracy had given the people the right to choose their leaders. In the past, bright uniforms had served the purpose of intimidating the enemy by making the soldiers stand out from their background, but also the officers' uniforms had made them stand out from the mass of soldiers. These hierarchical distinctions became less important in the move to modern democracy, as social background became relatively unimportant to the assertion of the right to vote or run for office. Kern (1994: 167–68) speaks of "a broad process of leveling older hierarchies in many areas of human experience beyond the social and political" and locates that process particularly among Cubists, who allowed foreground and background to interpenetrate each other and thus "democratized the picture surface."

To translate this into the scene in the Church of the Holy Sepulchre during the rite of the Holy Fire, it would be as if the carefully designated spaces between ethnic groups had been lost and people were allowed to mingle freely: no background, no hierarchy, and, above all, no waiting for access to the fire itself, which would be given freely to all at the same time from their own resources. The moment of silence would be replaced by a multitude of moments of alternative murmurs and pauses distributed—like the fire itself—widely and freely among those who had gathered. It would not be imposed by and relieved from the top by the archbishop but would well up, so to speak, from the laity, from the people themselves, as in a Quaker meeting. There would be no need to wait because no one would be standing on ceremony. The dangers of waiting too long are tragically symbolized in Jerusalem's monuments of the Holocaust. In their essay to which I have already referred ("The Israeli Memory of the

Shoah: On Symbols, Rituals, and Ideological Polarization"), Saul Friedlander and Alan B. Seligman (1994: 356–71) point out that for some years after the Holocaust in Nazi Germany it was widely understood among citizens of the modern state of Israel that there had been something shameful about the passivity of the Jews who had gone without a struggle to their deaths; only those who had fought, like the heroes of the Warsaw ghetto, were to be honored in sacred memory and to have a place with the other heroes of the nation. However, as the memory of the Shoah was included in national days of mourning and remembrance, it became less popular to make the distinction between those who had died passively and those who had fought to the death. The Shoah was included in the memory of all catastrophes such as the destruction of the Temple, the exile, and the Crusades linked symbolically with the historical redemption represented by the new state of Israel.

However, even on the Mount of Zion, the monuments commemorating the founders of the nation and the monuments commemorating the Holocaust are quite separate, the former being on the side of the hill facing Jerusalem and the latter facing the outside world. It is as if the monumental sites of Israel make the distinction between the nation's capacity to anticipate and overcome threats and to shape its environment, on the one hand, and the tendency to wait far too long for signs of divine redemption, on the other. The people and the state are enshrined separately (Friedlander and Seligman 1994: 362ff.).

At the heart of this distinction in holy sites on the holy hill, we are told, lies a fundamental difference in Israelite tradition with regard to waiting (Friedlander and Seligman 1994: 356ff.). On the one hand are the Chassidim, who have believed over the millennia that it is sacrilegious to take the power of the state into one's own hands; the redemption of Israel will come only when God determines to intervene in history. Until that day of redemption, the only posture incumbent upon the true believer is one of obedient and expectant waiting; the only question is "How long?" As Friedlander and Seligman (1994: 357) explain,

Indeed, during the centuries of Jewish dispersion, exile had no meaning in its relation to redemption and was mostly considered as a cathartic preparation for it. As the exile was a divine punishment, only God could terminate it, and so for the majority of Jews messianism had to be passive. The very dichotomy of historical delay and anticipated redemption resulted in strict warnings against any attempt to "hasten the End."

On the other hand are those who take a more active view of their role in God's purpose for Israel and see messianism as a historical possibility for those who are willing to take up the challenge of freeing Israel from its enemies and restoring divine rule to the nation. The split between these two traditions, of course, is far older than the Christian era, but it comes to a very visible point of catastrophic confrontation in the civil war of 66–73 C.E., following which the Gospel began to be written. No wonder that the traditional Israelite ambivalence toward waiting was inscribed in the Christian texts.

Rituals shape the sort of character that is well adapted to a contrived experience of an imaginary world. The last line of defense against social change is thus the body that has been socialized, trained, and accustomed to certain postures and habits: deference, demeanor, self-restraint and other social disciplines. The socialized body simply does not see or feel what might be discordant with the ritualized and hence taken-for-granted social order. It is blind, so to speak, but does not know that it does not see. Its orientation, in other words, is limited and predetermined.

Ritual, therefore, works only so long as people do not see that they are being inducted into a system in which some have more power and authority than others. It provides the illusion of common action, even while people are being inducted into a system in which legitimacy is monopolized by those in charge of the rituals themselves: "Ritualization sees the evocation of a consensus on values, symbols, and behavior that is the end of ritualization. It does not see the way in which the hegemonic social order is appropriated as a redemptive process and reproduced individually through communal participation in the physical orchestration of a variety of taxonomic schemes" (Bell 1992:110).

Further, the practice of ritual depends on signs and signals that are understood locally: "Ritual mastery implies that ritual can exist only in the specific cultural schemes and strategies for ritualization...em-

bodied and accepted by persons of specific cultural communities"
(Bell 1992: 107).

The institutional dilemma of the church is based on its ritual commitment to raising expectations of judgment, followed by verdict,
absolution, and suspended sentence, or to intensifying expectations
of redemption and release, to be realized only in an eschatological or
proleptic sense. Thus, the tension between the active and the passive
forms of waiting is a product of the Church's rituals. On the one
hand, individuals are told to wait with eager anticipation for the beginning of the end, a beginning that can be a bane or a blessing depending on one's faith or virtues. On the other hand, the Church
steps in as a source of protection against an end for which the believer
may not be ready. Thus, the Church claims its lord to be an effective
advocate with a determined judge or a healer whose blessings are a
foretaste of the final reconciliation of all things.

The Church is no longer a powerful religious community in a position to mobilize and to pacify its followers, to heighten expectations
and also to inure the participants to a long wait for satisfaction. To
create different kinds of waiting and then offer the solution to the
problem of waiting is possible only if the priesthood has a monopoly
on the definition of time.

The power of the priesthood, in turn, rests on the capacity of rituals to evoke presences and times that are far removed from the present and to deprive the participants of a sense of their own agency in
creating the world. Societies, then, are "auto-poietic" (Luhmann),
but because of ritualization they see themselves as being created by
external and superior forces: "Indeed, in seeing itself as responding
to an environment, ritualization interprets its own schemes as impressed upon the actors from a more authoritative source, usually
from well beyond the human community itself" (Bell 1992: 109–110).

To the extent that individuals are not aware of the effect of ritualized actions in creating and shaping a social system, they will be acting as dupes of the system that they are in the process of creating. It
may seem to them that the community is convening for their sake;
on the contrary, it is they who are being convened for the sake of the
community: "Ritualization does not see how it actively creates place,
force, event, and tradition, how it defines or generates the circum-

stances to which it is responding. It does not see how its own actions reorder and reinterpret the circumstances so as to afford the sense of fit among the main spheres of experience—body, community, cosmos" (Bell 1992: 109). Societies begin to lose their taken-for-granted order, however, as individuals become aware of the use of rituals for social control. Rituals begin to fail when they become obviously the instruments of manufacturing a consensus.

When ritual fails, the sabbath can be seen to have been made for humans, not "man for the sabbath," and the Temple becomes a place where the power of the people is expropriated for the use of consolidating the power and authority of a relatively privileged few. Societies becomes less ritualized as people openly discuss what the ritual is doing. Language is no longer subordinated to the command performances within the rite itself. Thus the giving of consent or the making of promises is then seen as a way of getting people voluntarily to take upon themselves the burden of duties, the respect for authority, and the rules for excluding others that are being impressed on them by the larger society.

The less ritualized a society becomes, the more individuals will be able to use language to reflect on the rituals themselves. In arguments during the Reformation over whether there is a real, a virtual, or only a symbolic presence in the Eucharist, the sheer fact of the discussion itself heralded an awareness that consensus is contrived and that the obligatory can be optional. Rituals begin to fail, then, as individuals begin to entertain possibilities that were unimaginable and imagine a world that was previously unthinkable. The sacred, ritualized order then becomes shaky; the Temple can be destroyed and rebuilt in three days. In the aftermath of the failure of ritual, people become increasingly able to associate with others who have hitherto been regarded as beyond the pale.

To summarize: ritual employs various schemes as instruments for knowing and appropriating the world. The deployment of these schemes both structures experience of the world and molds dispositions that are effective in the world so experienced. These structured and structuring experiences of the world appear to guarantee the reality and value of their underlying schemes by means of the sense of fit or coherence between the instincts of the socialized body and the environment in which it acts. (Bell 1992:115)

As a society becomes less effectively ritualized, the body begins to be liberated. Hence the lame walk, and the deaf hear. What people thought they saw then seems increasingly unreal, and they are no longer blind to the repression of their own senses and to the manipulation of their sense of reality by authorities whose legitimacy had been impressed on them in ritual. The experience is akin to waking up from a trance. When one wakes up, time seems to be running out, and one is eager to make up for lost time.

Under these conditions, the world seems to be "new." That is, the old world, in which certain things and people were excluded and feared no longer seems so threatening, and new opportunities are seen as though for the first time. People are living in a "new creation," and God has made "all things new." Further, what used to be taken for granted or regarded as necessary is now seen to be a matter of choice or even superfluous. The old law, so to speak, has been nailed to the cross.

SIX

Pilgrimage to an Earthly City

THE LOSS OF A providential viewpoint leaves us at the mercy of societies that are self-organizing and self-justifying. The span of history offers little consolation or challenge to such a system; the challenges come from the environment, which is full of threat and possibility at any given time. The long view remains a staple of political rhetoric, whereas decision making follows the polls and the quarterly report. Such societies offer little in the way of symbolic gratification to the individual who is seeking to find in the nation or larger society a personification of his or her values and commitments.

Such societies demystify the passage of time and leave individuals on their own to sort out their ultimate loyalties. As a result, individuals are not torn between this world and some other world that is the consummation of every hope and longing. On the contrary, one is left with the sense that time is the only arena for human struggle. That is, one is no longer torn between allegiance to an earthly or a heavenly city; most conflicts are more mundane, for example, between the city of one's origin and the one to which one has emigrated later in life. Many immigrants in fact do shuttle back and forth between the countries of their origin and later residence. Those who stay put still live in a welter of earthly allegiances and may indeed be divided by conflicts, say, between home and work. However, it is a minority who long for another world in the midst of this one; their spiritual disease is not inevitable or beyond secular cure.

In Christian tradition, however, the pilgrim is typically a person split between two very powerful allegiances. Christian, in *Pilgrim's Progress*, was torn between the church bells that reminded him of home and the appeal of the distant goal, the heavenly city. Dante, as the pilgrim seeking the beatific vision, was clearly a divided soul: one foot dragging behind as he placed the other firmly ahead of him on his way up the mountain trail that led to the gate of hell. Even in hell itself Dante as pilgrim was torn between a pity that would have had him linger among souls in anguish and Virgil's reminder that such pity was a foolish distraction from the way to the world above. To live in a providential universe was to be divided between an earthly and a more exalted allegiance.

Even in the seventh century, Richard Fletcher (1997: 93ff) has reminded us, there was a close association between a sense of pilgrimage and the missionary work of the Church; the Church in the world had urgent work to do. Especially the barbarians were waiting for the Church to civilize and redeem them. We can get a sense of that urgency from this story, originally told of Columba, the sixteenth-century Irish monk and missionary, by Adomnàn:

> At one time when the holy man (i.e., Columba) was making a journey on the other side of the Spine of Britain [Adomnàn's term for the Western Grampians, which divided Dalraida from Pictland] beside the lake of the river Ness, he was suddenly inspired by the Holy Spirit, and said to the brothers who travelled along with him: "Let us hasten toward the holy angels that have been sent from the highest regions of heaven to conduct the soul of a pagan, and who await our coming thither so that we may give timely baptism, before he dies, to that man, who has preserved natural goodness through his whole life, into extreme old age." Saying this, the aged saint went as fast as he could, ahead of his companions, until he came to the farmland that is called Airchartdan [Urquhart]. And a certain old man whom he found there, Emchath by name, hearing and believing the word of God preached by the saint, was baptised; and thereupon, gladly and confidently, with the angels that came to meet him he departed to the Lord. And his son Virolec also believed and was baptised, with his whole house.[1]

Of course, Fletcher retells this story to emphasize the connection between monks and mission, a point to which I will return in the next chapter. The monk Adomnàn, however, who was writing this story for the edification of the monks in the Iona community some years after the death of Columba, was more intrigued by the angelic presence, the point also that interests me here (Fletcher 1997: 95). Time was running out for the old man, but it was also the angels who were kept waiting.

There were other sources of temporal conflict in Patrick's life, but they were always intensified by the pressures of the world to come. He was torn between his sense of obligation to the Irish, among whom he had been captive, and his affection for his family in England, with whom he had just been reunited after years in captivity. In an earlier section of his *Confessio*, Patrick had told of what might in these days be considered a flashback to a period of trauma in his life, a painful recovery of the time when he as a young boy had been taken captive to Ireland and had spent many lonely years herding sheep in the hills:

> Again a few years later I was in Britain with my kinsfolk, and they welcomed me as a son and asked me earnestly not to go off anywhere and leave them this time, after the great tribulations which I had been through. And it was there that I saw one night in a vision a man coming from Ireland (his name was Victoricus), with countless letters; and he gave me one of them, and I read the heading of the letter, 'The Voice of the Irish', and as I read these opening words aloud I imagined at that very instant that I heard the voice of those who were beside the forest of Foclut which is near the Western sea; and thus they cried, as though with one voice: 'We beg you, holy boy, to come and walk again among us.' And I was stung with remorse in my heart and could not read on, and so I awoke.[2]

Note the remorse. It could well be that Patrick was filled with the sense of acute responsibility, even guilt, that is sometimes felt by those who have been able to survive a disaster or escape from prison, when others whom they had come to love had not been so fortunate. It could also be that Patrick was experiencing a sense of remorse in anticipation of a spiritual victory over those who had held him captive; after all, the name of the man bringing these letters was Victoricus. We cannot begin to do more than speculate, but it would be a mistake to underestimate the amount of spiritual agony that Patrick endured even after his escape from Ireland. In the same passage he goes on to speak of a spiritual agony that could not be expressed in words, whereas in this passage the man from Ireland arrives with "countless letters." That he had untold agony, and that his remorse may have been the conscious experience of far deeper emotions, is simply his own testimony. The point here is that an otherworldly dimension was added to the struggle between conflicting loyalties: the one loyalty being to his home, the other to those with whom he had once been a captive and who now laid on him the claims of the strongest affection. Patrick is, after all, the "holy boy." It is not only the future that is at stake; there is an eternal dimension to this engagement between his present and his past.

It may also be that this tug of war between an earlier and a later stage of his life was the theater in which he dramatized an even more personal schism within his psyche. Patrick reported the following dream:

> And another night (I do not know, God knows, whether it was within me or beside me) I was addressed in words which I heard and yet could not understand, except that at the end of the prayer He spoke thus: "He who gave His life for you, He it is who speaks within you," and so I awoke, overjoyed. And again I saw Him praying within me and I was, as it were, inside my own body, and I heard Him above me, that is to say above my inner self, and He was praying there powerfully and groaning; and meanwhile I was dumbfounded and astonished and wondered who it could be that was praying within me.[3]

Clearly, even in his dream, Patrick had been divided between what he recognized to be his "inner self" and a more authoritative voice, one that he identified with Christ and with the Holy Spirit, that could find the words for what would otherwise have been his untold agony. For Patrick the voice of spiritual authority prevailed, and he was the first Western Christian, Fletcher argues, ever to have extended the mission of the Church to the barbarians beyond the known reaches of Roman civilization. A heavenly voice, within the body but above the inner self, so to speak, was in a position to articulate the ineffable and to give voice to inner anguish. To internalize providence gave the soul a divine overseer, but it also created a split between a lower, "inner" self and a higher one that was conversant with the purposes of God.

This internal split in the pilgrim's psyche was a clear legacy of the Christian gospel, which celebrates the God who dwelt with us, Emmanuel. In the Incarnation there is no abode too humble for the Son of God, yet the Son of man has nowhere to lay his head. This world is good enough for God, and yet within it the Christian soul must undertake a journey into loneliness and alienation from the usual comforts of home and community. Moreover, the kingdom offered by Jesus is not of this world, and the Christian's true citizenship is always in heaven. As a result, Christians were internally divided by their allegiance to two worlds, this one and the other.

This tension intensified the meaning and significance of time, since one had to be simultaneously, as it were, in two spiritual places. The pilgrim therefore could not afford to rest but always had to press ahead to the kingdom, while nevertheless being attentive to signs and responsive to appeals for charity along the way. Dante got it right; this tension made one feel as if one were always about to be too late. Gauchet (1997: 130–31) reminds us that it is only partly true that

> whoever scrupulously followed the message delivered by the Incarnation became . . . beings inwardly freed from any worldly affiliation by their secret dealings with the extra-worldly god. This . . . does not fully take account of the dynamic tension inherent in the individualizing structural link between the here-below and the beyond, a tension crucial to the development of history. There is a dual tension, one in faith's relation to itself, and the other in its relation to external reality. These individuals inwardly isolated from the world were still outwardly subjugated to it, both as corporeal and social beings. They had to win their spiritual autonomy by first turning against that part of themselves

dependent on physical reality and controlled by it. Their individual liberty was won at the price of a personal split.

The "personal split" meant that one part of the self had to be held in abeyance, suppressed, even repudiated and repressed in order for the other to flourish; such psychological splits do indeed create a feeling as if part of one is dying or at least running late. This inner split and the concurrently agonized sense of time were acted out in the pilgrim's struggle against physical and social odds; the "world" became a place of distractions, temptations, and inevitable hindrance and delay. As Gauchet (1997: 131) goes on to remind us, "We find ourselves in a vicious circle of obligations: we must hold ourselves outside the world while admitting we live in it." The pilgrim, torn between these two sets of obligations, fully understood how some souls could find themselves in hell because, forgetting one set of obligations, they gave inordinate attention to the other.

Thus, there has been a shift in the meaning of the "temporal." In the past, the temporal order stood defined by its tension with the eternal order. The church, despite its tendencies to acquire "temporal" power, depended for its legitimacy entirely on its sources of authority in the "other world." There was a split in the order of things, corresponding to the "personal split" experienced by the pilgrim:

> From the outset, the division between spiritual and temporal allegiance attested by the Church and the hierarchical separation of the two powers, placed the Church far beyond the traditional relation of priestly and sovereign function. The Church did not arise from the harmonious cooperation of two spheres; its existence signified the breakdown of any possible organic connection between administering the world and concern with heaven. (Gauchet 1997: 133)

Hence, every pilgrimage was filled with a reminder of the tension between the two orders: the earthly city being a poor figure of the celestial one, and it was to the earthly city, whether Jerusalem or Rome, that the pilgrim must proceed. It is always the earthly city that is running out of time and that fails to recognize the time of its visitation by heavenly powers. Obligations to that city frequently compete with one's heavenly duties, even though the earthly ones are inevitable and inescapable.

In a more highly secularized society, however, the "dynamic tension" that afflicts the pilgrim gives way; the vicious circle is broken to the extent that one's temporal horizons stretch horizontally ahead without being interrupted, so to speak, by the vertical. It is difficult enough to be torn between past and future, without having constantly to obey a summons from other worldly obligations. The pilgrim may live in a present that stretches on indefinitely over an apparently barren or even arduous terrain without being interrupted by mountains pointing to a heavenward destination. The secular pilgrim may continue to feel the weight of the past, of obligation to the future, and of the appeals and demands of the present, but time pressures are neither relieved nor intensified by the prospect of eternity.

Thus, the nature of pilgrimage depends on what sort of society one is in. Turner himself noted that in modern societies, pilgrimage is quite a different affair than in societies that are more highly integrated and ritualized. In the past, he noted, pilgrimages had a beginning and an end. One started out with the sure and certain hope of arriving at a certain destination in time for the communal celebrations that reunited one with one's past and the larger society. In modern societies, he went on to note, pilgrimage becomes a way of life, without a timely beginning and a dramatic end. Life is in a perpetual liminal process that he called "liminoid." Limbo thus becomes a chronic social condition rather than a temporary condition.

One goes on a secular pilgrimage without being sure that one's destination matters from any providential viewpoint. In Britain, for instance, only about a quarter of the population still believe either in heaven or hell (Bruce 1996: 33). One is now exposed to the passage of time on one's own, to make of it what one will; relatively few believe in a second chance after death. On the other hand, relatively few believe in hell; if they do experience hell, it is in this life, when it becomes clear that it is too late to satisfy old longings or to undo past wrongs. Time is all the modern individual has.

Furthermore, in a secularized social order, one earthly city simply evokes another. Passaic, New Jersey, evokes Bombay for many of its Indian citizens. The Guggenheim in New York evokes the one in Balboa. Locally one is in the company of transnationals, and abroad one finds oneself in the company of those who sing the same songs, have the same movie idols, and butcher the same language. The recent sociological attention given to so-called transnational collectivities further underscores the notion that solidarity is decreasingly national in scope and origin and more likely to be based on ethnic or religious identities that transcend and often cross national boundaries. If pilgrimage represents the temporary convergence and partial interpenetrating of radically different social and psychological worlds, more individuals are increasingly likely to experience such conditions without going far from their local communities. If there are narcissistic satisfactions to be found in the social system, they are shifting, local, temporary, and cross-cultural.

Individuals thus have become increasingly separate from their institutional contexts; they come on their own terms, as it were, to their various roles. Voters become more independent, and patients pursue alternative therapies without the blessing or control of the medical establishment. It is a milieu in which the Gospel's imperative to physicians to heal themselves makes increasing sense; it is also a milieu conducive to belief in the Gospel's assurance to the sick that their own faith will make them whole. Individuals may make use of professionalized medicine, but they come to it not as supplicants or believers but as individuals taking an active role in their own cure and as independent minds asking their own questions. As personal intelligence and agency take the place of submission and credulity, neither authoritarian medicine nor clerical pronouncements can deprive individuals of the right or the responsibility to work out their existence on their own terms.

None of this is incompatible with belief in God. In fact, God also becomes just a matter of time. As Alverson (1994:95) points out, the notion of God as the divine clockmaker was "the ultimate in the culturally peculiar fetishization of time." A clockwork deity is no respecter of persons and has little regard for the vicissitudes of individual experience over time. Among Deists, the clockmaker deity was a reminder of the inexorable and apparently endless passage of time, a chilling prospect that inspired various attempts, such as Freemasonry, to reenchant the universe and to restore an idealized past.[4] The clockmaker sort of God puts a good face, as it were, on the passage of time, but it is not the face of a benign and actively interested providence.

Whereas an enchanted temporal universe can be full, as it was "once upon a time," a clockmaker deity's universe is empty of everything except duration (Alverson 1994: 67–68). It is therefore difficult for preachers or demagogues and politicians to call for sacrifice so long as time itself is seen as merely passing inevitably away. To urge upon individuals that they should take sacrificial action in the "nick of time" or when the "time is ripe" requires a temporal universe filled with heroic memory and anticipation. Any attempt to require a sacrifice of the self needs to suggest that there is a larger temporal framework in which no sacrifice is ever lost or unrewarded.

To demand that others link their personal fates with the destiny of the larger society and to disregard their personal needs or desires, it is necessary to evoke more than a time that "wears away" and takes all its sons and daughters to their graves; it is necessary to evoke a common belief in a shared time that enshrines collective memory. If a nation is to offer recognition for personal sacrifices, it is necessary collectively to look forward to a day that will heal and wipe away all the nation's—and the individuals'—tears. Secular societies that are visibly prone to the passage of time are therefore not likely to be able to summon the moral reserves of the population or to insist on more than the occasional sacrifice.

Under these conditions, there is literally no need for an institution that stores up a treasury of grace from which the penitent can draw for forgiveness. Neither is there any need for an institution that can pass on an authoritative interpretation of what one ought to believe for the good of one's own soul. Gauchet (1997: 137) puts it very succinctly: "Any claim by the Church to interpose itself between ultimate otherness and extreme inwardness becomes an absurd hoax, any communitarian bridge thrown across the abyss toward heaven seems an idolatrous misunderstanding of transcendence."

What is lost in this process of emancipating the individual, however, is the sense of a society that represents what is lasting about the individual and a history that takes into account the fate of the self. Because individuals are now left to their own devices to assuage their sense of loss, grief increasingly becomes private. Clocks no longer keep the times of the spirit but of the workplace. The rhythms of the public sphere reflect the demands of the fiscal or tax year far more than any collective season of mourning or thanksgiving. To be sure, there are public displays of grief, like the unrolling of a gigantic quilt in Washington, on which are sewn the names and mementoes of the thousands who have died thus far from AIDS. However, the quilt offers no permanent image of loss; it is rolled up and taken away to wait for another occasion. When even the public memorial of grief becomes occasional and temporary, one's own existence may also seem increasingly ephemeral. Behind Warhol's adage that each person has only fifteen minutes of fame is the realization one may have little more than fifteen minutes of immortality. The clock is running out even on one's life after death.

The last line of defense against the secularization of time is ritual.[5] Whereas rituals once evoked the past and foreshadowed the future, now—at least in modern societies—they are themselves temporary, improvised, contingent, alternative, experimental, trial, ad hoc, and hence emptied of collective hope and anticipation. That rituals provide only the illusion of action is therefore increasingly apparent even to the devotee. Because rituals themselves are temporary and experimental, the believer is painfully aware that the fleeting moments of liturgical transcendence are only for the time being; transcendence itself is simply a matter of time.

Note the transformation of ritual into a temporary expedient in Hare's play *Racing Demon*. You will remember my earlier discussion of the play, in which I focused on the character of the senior clergyman, Lionel, a rebel against time who keeps himself and others waiting far too long. You may also remember Tony, the young evangelical clergyman concerned about the fate of a young Jamaican woman, Stella. Tony wishes to contrive a service that would dramatize the urgency of the moment and change the future for a young woman, not embody a timeless order into which individuals may enter at their own pace, regardless of their command of religious language, and so on. In the character of Tony, Hare gives us the portrait of a clergyman who seems on the surface at least to be Lionel's opposite; certainly he is Lionel's rival for leadership of the parish. Tony is a rather ambitious young evangelical, who in earlier years had been a beer salesman and who now finds himself hawking higher spirits. Whereas Lionel seems oblivious to the slow but impending death of his wife and his parish, even while being apparently quite realistic about the pressure of time in his work, Tony is in a very real hurry to save others. No wonder that Tony soon grows impatient with Lionel for not doing more for Stella. Whereas Lionel prays with her, offers her friendship, and lets her go, Tony wants to make a big difference in her life and to bring her back to church the next Sunday with a promise that something might happen that would change her life:

> The statistics are appalling. We feel we've had a good Sunday if between us we attract one per cent. One per cent of our whole catchment area. All right, I know this is terribly vulgar, numbers aren't everything—it's the quality of the experience and so on— but I would have said, 'Look, madam, actually next Sunday we will perform an act of worship which it might do you some real good to attend." . . . I want a full church. Is that so disgraceful? I want to see the whole community all worshipping under one roof. That's what I want. And that's what I believe the Lord wants as well. I'm the junior member, this is my first parish, I've no right to bring this up, I can tell, we can go about our business, we can look at our schedules, but really if in three years we don't fill the churches on Sunday, I'm sorry, then I think we'll have failed. (Hare 1991: 16)

Tony clearly remembers a day in which people were expected not only to believe in God but to attend church, and not only to attend but to be members of the church in good standing. His imagined world is one in which, to put it more formally, the differentiation of identity from participation and of participation from membership has been reversed. Thus, Tony wants to fill the local church building in three years: a modern equivalent of a messianic promise to rebuild the Temple in three days. He also wants to take messianic action to rescue Stella. Unfortunately for Stella, he arrives too late to prevent her from being burned with scalding water by her aggressive husband. Thus, Tony attacks Lionel because Stella has become half-blinded by scalding water thrown at her by her husband: "It could have been prevented" (p. 48).

Added to this experience of chronic urgency is Tony's reluctance to draw a line between the possible and the impossible. The sense that life is full of infinite possibility passes for faith, whereas in fact it is an antidote to the feeling of powerlessness to prevent suffering and disaster. That antidote, like Real Ale, is the drive behind Tony's desire to save lives and souls with heroic and timely intervention. Explaining to the other clergy in the parish why he plans to complain to the bishop about Lionel's ineffective leadership, Tony says:

> What is this? The Civil Service? . . . Put in twenty years and then you can speak? . . . I went round to this woman's house . . . I experienced this feeling of utter powerlessness. The Church can do nothing in our parish except witness to suffering . . . And I'm afraid I no longer think that's enough. I'm tired of standing there, wringing my hands and saying, "Oh, this is dreadful . . ." (p. 49).

Tony is subject to the worst temptation of all; as his colleagues put it, he is tempted by "the illusion of action" (p. 54). Clearly, Tony is not willing to wait for twenty years until he is allowed to speak; indeed, for Tony, speech itself carries an urgency all of its own. Not only is he eager to speak his mind, but he is also eager to respond immediately to what he regards as a call for help from Stella—a call with the force of an oracle from God. Thus, in Tony we find a reactionary messianism cloaked under the modern language of a "policy" to deal with "cases" like Stella. We are therefore not surprised to find Tony eventually proclaiming that Jesus is the cure for AIDS.

The temptation to engage in the "illusion of action" would be irresistible for a man who, before his conversion, had been a member of the Film Society and had promoted Real Ale. Tony himself is not entirely real; even in the play he is a theatrical character living in a celluloid world. Indeed, there is a note of performance in Tony's character that makes much of what he says seem to be an act. He was until recently a beer salesman and a movie buff. His sense of reality, in other words, was never very strong. Once he used to be someone with plenty of time, "actually quite easygoing": "I spent all my time at the Film Society and running the Campaign for Real Ale. But now I can actually feel my sense of humour departing. It's gone . . ." (p. 20). Later, in expounding his faith for the benefit of those who do not see the possibilities for the future that are so exciting to Tony, he makes his case for intervening in the lives of others, and against reality, once and for all: "Two thousand years ago. There was an intervention. . . .

And when God did this, when he sent his own son, then he offered a model, it was a promise, if you like, to the rest of us, No one need be bound by the rules of reality . . ." (p. 69). Tony's distaste for reality, like his desire to intervene and rescue, and his need to fill the church with people who are for the time being missing, can be traced to the accident in which Tony's parents died as their car hit a patch of ice on a country road. At first, Tony tried to assuage his grief in a love affair with Frances, the woman who found Lionel dreamy and self-destructive. In a later encounter Frances reminds Tony that he used to wake up at night and make love to her, "Crying all the time." Tony recalls, in a voice still heavy with grief, "How can I have been so stupid? I used to try and find comfort in you . . . In your body. It was crazy. I realize now *I was wasting my time*" (p. 68; emphasis added). It is then that we learn that Tony has lost both his parents in an automobile accident, and that he had found in Frances something more than solace for an anguish that he has now turned into a passion for ministerial advancement as well as for rescuing all those whose lives are blighted or in jeopardy. Thus, he keeps Frances waiting for a commitment that never comes, even while he exhibits emblems of devotion to the poor, to the church, and particularly to the bishop.

In Tony, then, we have a character who takes up the several themes of a secular experience of time. He is clearly alien to institutions that once seemed timeless; indeed, for him the church is like any other institution that is subject to the constraints and passage of time. They have three years to fill the church or they will have failed. Clearly also Tony is engaged in a process of secret mourning. There is no shared memory of his parents, and the world as a result seems somewhat counterfeit. Ale has to be "real," and the world of films is taken for reality. In this world Tony is deathly afraid of wasting time, and though he may keep his lover, Frances, waiting, he himself can wait no longer. Indeed he lives out a messianic fantasy that he must come to the rescue in the nick of time to save the virgin mother.

There are many reasons that the world and the church may seem counterfeit and that one may feel that there is no time to waste. During infancy and childhood there may have been painful gaps between the timing of the infant's needs and the timing of parental responses: a lack of synchrony, which later is experienced as the feeling that time is running out and the world is not a reliable place. Early problems with timing may have been reinforced by later dreams of oedipal glory; the child thus may develop extraordinary impatience at having to wait to grow up. In addition to the pressure of oedipal strivings that may have made waiting seem intolerable, the child, like Tony, may have entertained grandiose notions of his or her prerogatives in life and have decided to suspend the "rules of reality." If so, the child's development remains incomplete, and the child continues to entertain fantasies of gaining adult stature and rewards without having to grow up (Chasseguet-Smirgel 1985:34).

In suspending the rules of reality, however, the child makes the world seem counterfeit; mundane requirements seem contrived and phony, and the real thing, the Real Ale, is all that matters. So begins the waste of time, as the young grow older and yet shun the present in order to hold on to a past in which they summon others, as though by magic, and wishes would come true. Note the vicious circle that comes from suspending the "rules of reality." Unable to cope with a sudden loss, like the death of Tony's parents, the child denies their total disappearance; then, because someone dear is missing, the world itself comes to seem unreal. Tendencies to live in an imaginary world make departure and death even more difficult to understand and accept, and the failure to say "goodbye" to the departed makes the world, in turn, seem even less real than before. There is a waste of time in attenuating emotional reactions—in thinning them out into smaller, medicinal doses—just as there is a waste of the present in holding on to the past. That is why Tony has not a moment to waste and must fill the church in three years.

Buying time, making up for lost time, borrowing time, stealing time: all these metaphors suggest that time is at one's magical disposal. Such views of time make it into "an external reality [that] exists corresponding to the infant's capacity to create" (Schiffer 1978:87). Thus, time can stand for the person one has lost or for the lost part of oneself. Anxiety over time may express feelings of remorse or satisfaction over lost or broken relationships. Indeed, as a transitional object, time becomes an extension of the self: something that one can manipulate, like turning back the hands of the clock. The more we make time into a transitional object, and the more we are subject to illusions, based on magical thinking, the more we try to manipulate time for magical purposes (Schiffer 1978:87).

Thus, magical thinking goes to work on time, turning it into a physical symptom, as if by holding back one's emotions, one could make time stand still. Conversely, the unconscious may go to work on time, as if one could recover an old love or romance by making up, as it were, for lost time. Those who confuse lovemaking with "making time" will inevitably bear an additional burden of time. To deprive time of its significance as a transitional object requires that one abandon magical thinking and various emotional strategies for "buying time" or "making up for lost time."

The paradox of secularization is thus relatively obvious. On the one hand, the tension between time and eternity that drove the pilgrim and the ascetic to undertake heroic spiritual challenges has been relaxed; one now lives in an indefinite duration, in which even the traditional symbols of transcendence are clearly temporal. Even liturgies and expectations of a millennial transfusion of divine grace are merely a matter of time. On the other hand, however, the internal struggle within the psyche continues; the soul is torn between a self that still stands on ceremony and believes in the capacity magically to alter the flow of time, and the self that knows that time is continually running out.

SEVEN

Passing the Test of Time

INFANTS WHO DISCOVER that the world is no longer in harmony with their own internal rhythms are "out of sync," as it were,
and in that sense may feel that they are late and running out of time,
when it is in fact the world that is not keeping pace with the infants'
rhythms and needs. Freud's friend and colleague, the Hungarian analyst Sandor Ferenczi (1995:83), noted what many analysts have since
argued, that there is a certain trauma in the discovery that the world
can be frustrating: an environment that is disappointing and unreli-
able, demanding and frightening. However, Ferenczi recognized
that such frustration has a purpose; it makes the child able to develop
the sort of character that has a chance of making it in the world.

If we are to find a general, pervasive cause for arrested development in the individual's orientation toward time, then, it will need
to be precisely in such ordinary, nearly universal experiences of childhood. Nonetheless, Ferenczi argued that a very early split does occur
in the psyche, between the part of the child that seeks the continuous
and uninterrupted access to sources of support and security, and the
part of the child who is ready to be weaned, to cooperate with toilet
training, and to make allowances for parents who do not come on
time. Take weaning, for example: "In particular, it may be assumed
that a splitting occurs at this stage. The organism has to adapt itself,
for example, to the painful realities of weaning, but psychic resist-

ance against it desperately clings to memories of an actual past and lingers for a shorter or longer period in hallucination, I am still loved the same as before (hallucinatory omnipotence). All subsequent disappointments, later on in one's love life, may well regress to this wishfulfillment" (Ferenczi 1995:83). The translator of this passage, Michael Balint (1992), has since gone on to publish his discussion of what he calls "the basic fault": an awareness that there is a fundamental split in the psyche and a longing for the restoration of the old self that could take so much continuously for granted. Balint notes particularly that individuals engage in protracted mourning for this lost self because the verbal cure of analysis does not readily touch a split in the psyche that occurred before the infant knew how to speak. There is here a grief, as St. Paul puts it, "too deep for words."

Ferenczi (1995: 112–13) notes that the *fear of being alone* (Ferenczi's italics) can produce radical changes in the psyche and at least temporarily paralyze the will. The attempt to recover the lost matrix of the self in hallucination is an early example of the paralysis of the will that results from the fear of being alone. In this case the child is temporizing by imagining that the past is not completely over. As Ferenczi points out, however, there is a price to be paid for this form of temporizing. Later losses weigh more heavily on the psyche and are felt more keenly because they remind the child of the first time that a dream came to an end. Thus, some individuals will say, if asked, that they seem always to have been peculiarly saddened when certain things came to an end. They may always have had long memories; perhaps their memory of an earlier period of unfettered satisfaction has not died, even if it is only the memory of a hallucination. They may always have had good imaginations, capable of enjoying the sensation of being loved even when they were being ignored. On the other hand, they also know that they have indeed lost something; their world has been shattered, and with it there has been a fundamental split in their psyche: Balint's "basic fault."

It takes an act of will to accept this original loss and the primary splitting of what was then the infantile ego. That is why so many societies have rituals, like baptism, that require the individual to affirm an adult being that lacks—and will not seek to recover—primary attachments at least in their original form. Otherwise the earlier self, with its infantile longings, remains alive and present—in a good psychological position from which to convince the later self that its satisfactions and achievements are partial and disappointing. One then becomes vulnerable to the punishment dreams that Freud has described in such telling detail, for example, the examination dream that makes the adult dreamer suffer, at least for a moment, the anguish of not having been on time for the successful completion of a critical test.

Religion may then offer a respite from such an internal quarrel, along with the prospect of a heaven on earth and of a salvation that recovers such an unmediated relation to the world, but the price of accepting such a promise is the surrender of the autonomous self and of the will. That loss of will may be sanitized as a form of submission to the divine, but it in fact entails the death of the center of one's own being. While religious ritual may thus seek the "rebirth" of a person through an act of renunciation of the "archaic matrix," it then takes away that will by legislating new acts of self-sacrifice.

Until one, through an act of will, accepts the primary loss of a self that was enshrined in the original matrix, one may continue to feel as if one has a basic flaw, an original sin. Because of this flaw, one will continue to feel that one is late, in both senses of the word. One may spend a great deal of energy in trying to stay current and in keeping up with "the times." On the other hand, one will carry a chronic sadness about a world that one has lost. One refuses to know and accept the fact that it is too late to recover the infantile world of unmediated access to the source of one's being. It is therefore difficult, if not impossible, to allow the longing for such a restoration to wither and die. To continue to mourn the loss of that original paradise, the "archaic matrix," however, is to live in a chronic hell of one's own.

The residues of the longing for primitive attachment underlie the well-known examination dream, in which one is back in school and late for an examination that one must pass if one is to graduate. In the examination dream the dreamer is suddenly confronted with the passage of time. It is as if he or she had been daydreaming, lost in reveries of some sort. There is therefore a rude awakening when one discovers that it is late in the academic year and that one is due to take an examination. The dreamer may therefore go into a panic at the thought of being unable to graduate, since on some level the dreamer is aware that he or she is an adult who has been claiming for years to have graduated and earned the proper degree. One must therefore still take and pass the examination if one is to satisfy one's desire to enter into the world of adult gratifications. On the other hand, it is also too late for the dreamer to find and take the exam: too late in the semester, and too late in the day. One is too late, as it were, from the very beginning. Indeed, the examination dream makes the passage of time into an exquisite form of torture, as the dreamer finds it difficult to get the necessary books, to prepare for the exam, to locate the site of the test, and to catch up with other students who are already taking the dreaded test. No wonder that, on waking up from the examination dream, dreamers widely report their feelings of relief.

It is customary to interpret that relief as being due to the discovery that the dreamer's degrees are not a fraud (Kafka 1979:437). However, I would interpret that relief as the end of the "death agony" of the earlier self. Of course, the adult self is relieved to know that he or she did graduate, but there is another and, I would argue, a more intense relief that comes from the earlier self's having received a stay of execution. In the dream the earlier self does indeed torment the adult dreamer by claiming not to be ready to take and pass this critical examination, but the dream also comforts the earlier self by suggesting that this step toward separation from the alma mater will never have to take place. Of course, the dream does not express this reprieve directly. It is postponed until the moment of waking up, when the adult dreamer realizes that the dream was "just a dream." The residue of relief, however, is due not merely to this waking realization that one has indeed passed one's examinations but to the fulfillment of the unconscious wish not to graduate, that is, not to leave the alma mater. The past remains very much alive for the one who has had an examination dream. Consciously one has graduated into adulthood, but unconsciously one still lives in the embrace of the alma mater.

Those who focus entirely on the developmental issues in the dream may not see it as a subtle triumph for a part of the self that refuses to die. In her analysis of such dreams, for instance, Chasseguet-Smirgel (1985:34) distinguishes between those of the "pervert" and of the "neurotic":

It seems to me that this material shows how the pervert seeks to obtain matriculation without having to pass the exam, contrary to the neurotic who, in my experience, seeks to sit the examination again for fear of having obtained the diploma without deserving it. The neurotic attempts conciliation of his being with his seeming, whereas the pervert contents himself with make-believe. Time, as a dimension of life, is rejected by the pervert.... Recognition of obstacles, temporality, and reality are one and the same thing.

Chasseguet-Smirgel's analysis of the examination dream sees it more as a sign of arrested development than the struggle of a moribund part of the self to postpone its own death. Thus what she calls the perverted and the neurotic are simply different stages of development: different manifestations of the earlier self, each offering a clue as to what stage of development is being involved. The younger self's fear of being late, in the sense of being dead, may paralyze the will from letting go of the earlier, infantile longings for the comfort, continuity, and satisfaction of the original matrix.

If, as Chasseguet-Smirgel points out, "Recognition of obstacles, temporality, and reality are one and the same thing," an authentic way of being-in-time depends on one's ability to know when it is too late to satisfy certain longings and to accept that limitation. The psychology of hell, however, does not bring such acceptance. Those in Dante's hell know full well that they cannot revise the past or undo the damage they have done to others or themselves, but they are not yet reconciled to their fate or able to allow old passions to subside. Instead, they remain consumed in their desire or rage. Thus, Chasseguet-Smirgel's notion of a perverted character appears to be an earlier stage of the self more unwilling than the neurotic to accept the demands of reality—and more unwilling therefore to die.

Rather than work with a simple split between the perverted and the neurotic, I would prefer to think of a spectrum along which individuals would vary in their orientations to time. Toward the far left end of the spectrum are those who altogether reject the tests of time for the self. This is where the "ahistorical" persons reside; they live in an imaginary, timeless world of their own, where they do not need to learn anything. So far as is possible, they imagine that they remain within Chasseguet-Smirgel's "archaic matrix" of mother and child, where there is indeed plenty of time. Those at the far left end of the spectrum represent an earlier self that has managed to create a psychic paradise for itself where it can be immune to the pangs of temporal experience.

Somewhat to the right of this end of the spectrum would be the pervert, who prefers not to take the test of time and would avoid indefinitely any test of his or her own powers and limitations. Whereas the ahistorical person has abdicated time and thus has forfeited the opportunity to choose to take the tests of time, the pervert, instead of alternating between the world of fantasy and that of reality, actually makes the choice to avoid such tests. Instead of earning the usual credits associated with mastery by becoming an apprentice, the pervert mixes and matches, switches channels, as it were, and thus employs creativity to redefine the "reality-principle." Thus the perverted, Chasseguet-Smirgel notes, are likely to be very adept in crossing the usual boundaries between various domains. They exercise choice in the act of not respecting the usual boundaries precisely because they prefer to be agnostic about their own limitations.

The agnosticism of the perverted can prove dangerous. Before being tricked by his own fascination with the lovely angelic lads who were attending the grave of Faust and waiting for his soul to emerge, Mephistopheles declared that "such juvenile-androgynous bumbling \ is what the sanctimonious enjoy" (Goethe 1984:295, *Faust* 2, 2, ll. 687–688). Shortly after these same angels transport Faust's soul, Mephistopheles laments that he—"a seasoned devil"—could have been so easily fooled, (Goethe 1984:298, *Faust* 2, 1, l. 838). For the perverted character, it is presumably never too late to satisfy old longings or fulfill even the most outrageous aspirations; thus, to be suddenly confronted, as was Mephistopheles, with the fact that the game is lost is a very rude awakening indeed.

Let me repeat that this imaginary spectrum covers stages of development: not character types so much as earlier selves that may seek to punish the adult self for leaving them behind to suffer a slow death in relative psychological oblivion. The punishment takes the form of trying to convince the adult self that it is the adult who is running out of time, not the earlier self. Thus, as Chasseguet-Smirgel points out, the examination dream for the neurotic represents a sense of obligation to take the tests of time but a lack of confidence in being able to graduate. It is therefore necessary for the neurotic to take the test over and over again. Similarly, one may wish to engage in a Nietzschean struggle for self-mastery: a never-ending struggle, in fact, since the past eternally returns. For the neurotic it is also never too late to take the tests that qualify one for adulthood and mastery, but those tests must be taken repeatedly. Thus, the earlier self seeks to prevent the adult from having the satisfaction of graduation.

In these characters we therefore find various degrees of resistance to the fundamental experience of time: an unwillingness to accept that it is too late to fulfill certain longings or realize certain aspirations. The neurotic works at being-in-time harder than the pervert, who is more willing than the ahistorical character to face some of the constraints of time. All of these earlier stages of the self, however, compromise with reality in the sense of making a deal or "coming to terms" with time rather than fully accepting the verdict of the adult self that it is time for them to die.

Along this hypothetical spectrum, just to the right of the neurotic we find the "masochist." This character only pretends to struggle against the temptations to return to the protections of the "archaic matrix"; entertaining the fantasy of an eventual exaltation to paradise lies at the heart of masochism. On the surface, no one is more dedicated to accepting the passage of time than the masochist, who is burdened by schedules and appointments, and who knows that there will be no joyful reunion with the beloved prior to the end of time. Rainer Maria Rilke (1997:87) thus starts one of his poems on a brave note, as though he had fully come to terms with the separation from the original paradise and was now ready to take time on its own terms:

> You the beloved
> lost in advance, you the never arrived,
> I don't know what songs you like most.
> No longer, when the future crests toward the present,
> do I try to discern you. All the great
> images in me—the landscape experienced far off,
> cities and towers and bridges and un-

suspected turns of the path
and the forcefulness of those lands
once intertwined with gods:
all mount up in me to signify
you, who forever eludes.

"Lost in advance" states it precisely.

The masochist, I would argue, is thus tormented by the residues of an infantile self that experienced an original loss. That infantile part of the self has been split off but is remembered, and it continues to mourn, as though a part of the self had died. I will return to that point in the conclusion of this chapter, but here it is worth noting that this original loss, experienced by the infantile self, transforms all later perceptions into reminders of something that is indeed missing: as Rilke put it, "you, who forever eludes." The world—in the light of the original separation at birth—now looks like a paradise that has been forfeited: "lands once intertwined with the gods." For the adult haunted by this infantile self, life after birth is indeed like a separation from the original paradise; the world lacks a certain enchantment and a vital presence.

It is too late for the masochist to recover the sense of that original paradise, but the longings persist and can be experienced with renewed intensity. That experience, however, always comes with a reminder that there has been an abrupt separation that entailed at least a partial loss of the self. Rilke (1997:87) concludes the poem quoted earlier in this way:

Ah, you are the gardens!
With such hope I
watched them! An open window
in the country house—, and you almost
stepped out pensively to meet me. I found streets,—
you had just walked down them,
and sometimes in the merchants shops the mirrors
were still reeling from you and gave back with a start
my too-sudden image. —Who knows if the same
bird did not ring through both of us
yesterday, alone, at evening?

His own image in the mirror is "too-sudden," as though his reflection reminded him of the abrupt arrival of birth itself. That arrival also signifies the absence of the woman whose presence once made him feel as if he were in a land "interwined with gods." At birth, in infancy, and as though in repeat performances through one's life, self-discovery comes at the price of a sudden and irremediable loss of the prior self and its more or less enchanted milieu.

Note that the mirrors remind the poet of this loss, even at the same moment that they remind him of his own presence. Rilke arrives always, and everywhere, too late for the sort of "mirroring" for which he longs: the mutual interplay of presences that was once associated with the original matrix of infancy. It is not too late for him to desire—even yearn for—such a happy reminder of his own existence within the matrix, but it is forever too late for him to realize that desire. His self was lost in advance because it remained captive to the earlier enchantment of the original matrix. Therefore, despite all the strenuous searching, the careful exploration, and even pilgrimage itself, the self remains "you the never arrived." The masochist thus turns initial loss into a way of life that makes the world seem promising and yet counterfeit, while the self remains always on the way but fated never to reach its destination.

Religion alone offers the possibility of a secondary sort of enchantment that recapitulates the original matrix. In a short poem composed the following summer Rilke (1997:89) writes:

> See the carefree insect, how it plays, its whole world
> the sheltering womb.
> Nature, when it was sketched, received it, bore it,
> and bears it now—, and in that same
> motherspace it lives and spends
> its intimate time, frisking in the joyful
> body like a small Saint John.
> Whereas the mammal even as it suckles stares
> all eye.

To be alone in the world is to know by sight that one's nourishment comes from the outside; thus, Rilke's attempt through images of cities and towers, bridges and gardens to recover a sense of the presence of the world he had lost. Such an existence is an alienated one, separated by space from what it yearns for, as well as by time. To live by sight, as Paul put it, is not to have faith. Thus, faith comes only— for Paul and for Rilke—through hearing. Only if a birdsong rang "through both of us" at the same moment could his separation be borne, a reminiscence, perhaps, of the infant's experience of sounds that—heard from the womb—did indeed ring through both mother and child: the sound of providence.

Thus, the masochist endures the prospect of an indefinitely long struggle for the foreseeable future by anticipating ecstasy at the end. In the end, like Faust or Dante, he or she will be transported by a beatific vision of the queen of heaven. In the meantime, however, the masochist is likely to engage the future with grim determination. No wonder that masochists continue to lack confidence in having "arrived" so long as their earlier selves long for their original matrix and hanker after some sort of transcendence over time.

It is therefore difficult to know when someone is actually refusing to engage the present while allowing the past to slip away. Those who seem to be most determined to make progress may in fact be spinning their wheels in a repetitive effort to repeat the early frustrations and satisfactions of infancy. Certainly the masochist is typically engaged in dreams of providential triumph or rescue while undergoing lengthy privation and arduous effort in the apparent service of progress. Some individuals have been known to turn waiting into a way of life in which they act out, day after day, their identification with their parents. Altman (1957: 512, 518) refers to "the oedipal genesis" of waiting as a means of "outwitting and outwaiting" the rival parent or of keeping hope alive for access to the parental object of one's longing. Such a person is afraid of being late, in the sense of being unable to fulfill certain desires; to arrive in time, however, would mean that one could indeed fulfill strivings that are dangerous and illicit. Thus, the masochist typically seeks to delay the passage of time while engaging in attempts to make progress.

For the masochist, there is some virtue, then, in running late, since to arrive would force a test of one's oedipal powers. Since in this rivalry there are dangers of retribution if one actually acts on one's desires, waiting thus serves as a defense against the aggressive aspects of oedipal passions (Altman 1957:515). The critical factor is whether one has laid the past sufficiently to rest to be able to enter into the present on equal rather than superior terms to others without rebelling against the indefiniteness of the present, without dreams of eventual glory and retribution, and without consigning others to a past that one imagines that one has left behind and transcended. To live in the indefinite present in the full knowledge that time is running out, it is indeed necessary to relegate the past to "history." To create the past, in this sense, it is also necessary to know that one will still have something to show for the self in the present: a self that has "arrived."

Just beyond masochism is another character somewhat more reconciled to reality and to the passage of time than the masochist. Whereas the masochist still entertains dreams of future triumph and ecstatic reunion, for the "nostalgic" the search is fruitless. There is nothing to wait for and no pilgrimage to undertake. What one has lost is more real for the nostalgic than what remains. Whereas the masochist continues to struggle, if only with mock heroism, against the seductions of the past, the nostalgic simply laments their loss. Remember that the dedication to *Faust* begins with a voice lamenting,

> I feel the spell of long-forgotten yearning
> for that serene and solemn spirit realm . . .
> I feel a sense of dread, tear after tear is falling,
> my rigid heart is tenderly unmanned—
> what I possess seems something far away
> and what had disappeared proves real.
> (Goethe 1984:1, *Faust*, Dedication, ll. 25–26, 29–32)

Eventually it is Mephistopheles who can lament that what he has lost, the soul of Faust, proves far more real than the yearnings and the illusion of love that had distracted and unmanned him, "a seasoned devil." In that sense *Faust* is a vast exorcism of the nostalgic: an attempt to split off the yearning and lamenting part of Faust's psyche in order to save the soul still capable of rapture. The nostalgic are willing to allow the adult self to acknowledge the passage of time; they know that it is too late for them to recover what they once thought they possessed but now seems "something far away." Nonetheless, for the nostalgic, as for Goethe, "what had disappeared proves real." The nostalgic lament without being reconciled to the passage of time.

Still further along the spectrum, just beyond the nostalgic, is what I would call merely the "serious" approach to the tests of time in the everyday world. Here the individual is close to accepting that it is too late to make up for lost time, to undo old damages, and to satisfy ancient longings. In hell Dante was constantly under the tutelage of time, Virgil being the source of constant reminders to make the most of each moment. The substantial character of Dante in hell was contrasted with that of the shades; Dante's feet left prints on the ground, whereas the shades' presence lacked gravity. To acquire gravitas one must always face the agendas, schedules, and deadlines that embody what Freud called the "reality-principle."

No longer mere journeymen and parvenues, no longer masochistic or nostalgic, the serious are resolute about time. However, notwithstanding that they know that it is too late to fulfill them, the serious still entertain, however covertly, certain die-hard desires. Like Dante in hell, the serious therefore have a certain pity for those who are in anguish over the past, an anguish intensified by persistent desire that adds insult to the injuries of time. For the serious, then, to miss a deadline may mean much more than simply a failure to satisfy certain temporal demands but may signify something more ominous. For Freud, being late meant a variety of lapses: an inability to catch up with rivals; a failure to reach the bed of a dying friend, whose friendship was supposed to last forever; the psychological punishment for the imaginary crime of having eliminated rivals and superiors; and the feeling of having been mortified by a rebuke from a superior. Furthermore, as the word suggests, a "deadline" symbolizes the finality of death itself. Instead of fleeing from the reality of that final deadline, like the ahistorical and the perverted, or seeking to score psychological or moral victories over death, like the neurotic and the masochist, and instead of entertaining certain illusions and a nostalgia for "the immortals," the serious lack delusion. They know that they too will be irreversibly late, even though their longing for transcendence over time persists.

Thus, the spectrum I have outlined suggests variations in the rebellion of the earlier self against the passage of time. At the far left of the spectrum the experience of time is relatively tranquil, passive, and disengaged; indeed, time itself seems to be on hold. As one moves further to the right along the spectrum the individual is more actively and intensely engaged either in making up for lost time or in anticipating the future. Tranquillity yields to turmoil. The sense that time is passing one by yields to efforts to make up for lost time or to get somewhere in time. The regressive desire to recover the lost timelessness of the womb or of infancy becomes submerged within more active strivings to avoid being late. Orientation to the past is hidden within a more active engagement with the present and the future. The attempt to transcend suffering from unfulfilled desire becomes more transparent as it becomes more hopeless.

The rebellion against the passage of time is evident throughout the spectrum, as individuals engage in a number of strategies, more or less obviously magical in nature, to transcend, preempt, forestall, or anticipate the passage of time. The unbearable prospect, which is death itself, becomes more apparent toward the right end of the spectrum; there the individual is more directly confronted with the prospect of being "late" in both senses of the word.

Furthermore, any individual may move along the points in this spectrum during the course of a normal day or week. A diary of one's experience of time might record moments of daydreaming, in which one was oblivious to the passage of time, as well as moments of rude awakening in which one faces a test of one's abilities and limitations. One's response to such a test may vary from a playful tendency to change the rules to an anxious willingness to prove oneself. In the course of a normal day one may shift from moments of resigned longing for old attachments to a grim determination to persevere in the pursuit of a final vindication or of reunion with one's old flames. One may be overly serious during a day about keeping appointments and meeting deadlines, or one may become simply matter of fact about doing what one can in the time available.

EIGHT

Buying Time
Masochism, Continued

I F ONE IS FULLY TO experience the passage of time, one must be prepared to discipline what Freud called the "pleasure-principle." According to that principle, one refuses to experience emotions in all their intensity. One attenuates them, simultaneously holding on to pain and thinning it out in a sort of "attenuation" over time. The individual thus is stretching out both pleasure and pain in order to experience them both in tolerable doses, too much of either being overwhelming to the psyche. Medicinal doses of pleasure and pain, as it were, are preferable to an experience of intense sadness or joy. The psyche protects itself, then, by thinning out emotional experience. However, attenuation also means holding on to the original feeling rather than letting it go. That is why the masochist may seem to be savoring a pleasure rather than consummating it; masochists like to have their cake and to eat it, too. In other words, masochists perpetuate the pleasure of having cake by not finishing their portion; in this way they avoid the guilt or responsibility for the destruction that results from consuming something completely. Thus, by stretching out pleasure, one can hold on to it in a diminished form and avoid being overwhelmed by the intensity of experience.

To attenuate is a way, then, of temporizing, of "buying time" for the self to experience in smaller doses certain emotions that threaten to destroy the psyche. The result of this partial anesthetic, however, is that one exists in one's own psychic limbo, unable to relinquish entirely a split-off part of oneself. To quote Ferenczi (1995:88) one might say that "a greater or lesser part of them is dead, or killed, and is dragged around as a lifeless, that is nonfunctioning, burden."

The tendency of the masochist is to postpone living in order to postpone dying. However, one then begins to feel as if one is missing the boat, so to speak. Complete satisfaction remains elusive, and one is likely to feel late—delayed or held back—in an important but perpetual journey. So long as the experience of completion or consummation remains indefinitely in the future, it is inevitable that one will feel anxious about time: anxious, perhaps, that one will be late for an important connection.

None of this is novel. Freud, in the same essay in which he speaks of the "mysterious masochistic trends of the ego," points out that time is of the essence of the feeling of pain or pleasure. It is important to quote him in order to make the point more exactly; speaking of what constitutes the difference between pleasure and its opposite, Freud (1961:2) argues that "the factor that determines the feeling [of pleasure or unpleasure] is probably the amount of increase or diminution in the quantity of excitation *in a given period of time*" (Freud's italics). Thus, it is not merely a question of whether the individual is feeling more or less excitement but whether the excitement is experienced as being too much for the psyche at the moment. It is the moment— the amount of time—that determines whether or not the individual can cope with the excitement. Thus, to stretch out the excitement is a way of making it tolerable, as well as a technique for conserving the original experience, whether of pain or pleasure. The moment is stretched out—attenuated—and lends a sense of the momentous to what would be the ordinary—and momentary—experience of time.

Instead of accepting time with all its limits and proscriptions, individuals often are tempted to foreshorten their time perspectives. In so doing they play imaginary games with time. Some, for instance, revisit the scene of a once-fantasized crime or of a traumatic threat to their personal security; Freud spoke in this connection of a "compulsion to repeat." This compulsion is found, he argued, not only in neurotics but in normal people who seem to have the same sort of troubles over and over again, whether or not they seem actively involved in producing them (1961:22ff.). There is a real conflict, Freud argued, between the reality-principle and the pleasure-principle. The latter brooks no opposition and thus cannot face directly a point of pain or conflict, whereas the reality principle "does not abandon the intention of ultimately obtaining pleasure, but it nevertheless demands and carries into effect the postponement of satisfaction, the abandonment of a number of possibilities of gaining satisfaction and the temporary toleration of unpleasure as a step on the long indirect road to pleasure" (Freud 1961:4). It is therefore difficult to distinguish a self-destructive character from one that is simply well adapted to the demands of the world by being persistent, self-directed, and hard working.

There is a good reason that it should be so difficult to distinguish the pleasure- and the reality-principles from each other. They are both conservative, designed to protect the self. The pleasure-principle protects the self from internal dangers. Too much excitement "*in a given period of time*," as Freud put it, threatens the self with an explosion from within. Thus the pleasure-principle "buys time" for the psyche by stretching the stimulation out over longer periods, even while holding on to the original impulse toward satisfaction. That is why I stress that attenuation has more than one meaning: not only a thinning out but a holding on to the original impulse or stimulation, at the cost of consummating the longing and satisfying the impulse. One is therefore always running late in the search for satisfaction while appearing to obey the demands of time.

To attenuate, moreover, one can go backward in time rather than forward. When someone dies, for instance, it is not unusual to react to the shock by feeling that one could—even should—have foreseen the coming of the end. It is as if one could set back the clock and thus buy time. By imagining that one still has time in which to anticipate and thus cushion or even forestall the blow, one can hope to diminish the intensity of the original shock. Attenuation can thus include a mental passage backward in time not only to thin out the intensity of experience but to engage in what I will call *retrospective foresight*. It is as if one can imaginatively circumvent death or tragedy by going back in time in order to keep open the possibility of a relationship to the one who has died. In this refusal to admit that time does indeed run out, we see the crucial difference between the pleasure-principle and the reality-principle. The pleasure-principle will not foreclose on certain possibilities, whereas the individual who is dominated by the reality-principle can say "No" and "Goodbye." The individual who can thin out the experience of loss over a larger stretch of imaginative time seeks, in the fictitious world of the unconscious, to buy time; the payment for this imaginary purchase is to protract the experience of grief over a long period of time, perhaps even over a lifetime.

The belief in providence arises from prolonged spiritual struggles whenever individuals attenuate their experience of suffering to make it bearable and to delay a final separation from prior association and experience. As I have noted, the old self puts up a series of defenses against being consigned to the past, familiar strategies used as a last-ditch defense against being left permanently behind. One of these defenses, as I noted in the previous chapter, is simply to attack the emergent self as a newcomer, an arriviste or parvenu, to use Freud's terms. Another familiar defense is the examination dream, now used to punish the emergent self for premature attempts to graduate and to leave the old self to die. Later in this chapter I will discuss Freud's notion of a primary masochism, which may well refer to precisely this final struggle of the old self to remain undifferentiated from its original matrix.

Like a survivor of some terrible disaster, the emergent self may therefore find itself subjected to the most compelling appeals. The sense that time is running out, for instance, has been the code by which moribund parts of the self have signaled their distress, parts that have been numbed, suppressed, mortified, or split off from the rest of the self. It is these parts of the self that seek to delude the emergent self into feeling as if it is running out of time. As the individual begins to emerge with a firmer possession of the psyche and a more substantial sense of the self, the moribund, former self may seek to convince the adult self that it is the latter who is running late and who must make up for lost time. All these strategies, I am suggesting, are in the service of attenuating pleasure, thinning out the experience of painful separation and loss, and of holding on to earlier forms of the self.

The adult self may have to relinquish hope of fully recovering parts of the self that have been lost to abuse or other forms of mortification. The memory of victimization is particularly difficult in this regard, since at the time of the abuse the individual's will may have been poorly developed or the psyche immobilized by fear and enchantment. Memories of abuse are thus difficult to recover since so much of the self was often numbed at the time, and the abused child remembers only his or her perceptions of the abuser as someone in great pain and need. For the same reason, that is, the fantastic and partial nature of early experience, it is easy even for well-meaning, let alone unscrupulous, practitioners to induce a false memory of abuse. Still, an earlier paralysis of the will can be offset by an adult decision to close the psychological case and consign it fully to the past. Only with a clear sense of the distinction between the present and the past is it possible for an act of the will to let go of the prospect of imaginary satisfaction.

Otherwise, the search for the lost self becomes a romance with death: a masochistic flirtation with the dissolution of the boundaries of the self. That sort of psychological brinkmanship may reflect an attempt to recover enchanting others and old loves, or it may reflect the pressure of overwhelming impulse and of despair at ever recovering former parts of the self that are now "late" in every sense of the word. Thus, the discovery of the unconscious can initiate a preoccupation with the self that becomes habitual, unrelenting, interminable, and self-destructive. The knowledge that it is too late to satisfy old longings and to recover some aspects of the self can itself intensify the conviction that one is fundamentally flawed unless one comes to a sense of one's own being-in-time and of the solidity of one's inner self.

For Freud there was always an internal division or some war between rival instincts. I am arguing that this division represents the conflict between the emergent self and the self that is becoming moribund. The emergent self seeks to gain autonomy from—and yet seeks to recover—the older self, just as Freud, in his dreams, summoned back the "ghosts" of his former selves, in the guise of old friends and colleagues, only to dismiss them again. These aspects of himself were clearly moribund but not yet dead; hence, they were "late." Conversely, the former self accuses the emergent self of being an arriviste, a mere journeyman who has not mastered the craft of adulthood or stood the test of time, a student who has not yet taken and passed the tests necessary for graduation.

I would speculate that the reason the earlier self is allowed to continue to torment the later self is that the later, emerging self still needs a foil against which to exert itself. The need for such a foil, I would further speculate, is due to the original experience of the self in the womb. Certainly, in the womb, the self could only be experienced through what Ferenczi calls a "counterpressure." The tissues of the mother's body, the fabric of early care, the close presence of others: all these provided a matrix in which the substance of the surrounding world coalesced with the experience of the self. Thus, until the emerging self gives up the need for these counterpressures it will always be subject to the torments of the earlier self and vulnerable to the emotional seduction of the infantile matrix. For the self to develop, however, requires that one acquire a spiritual center that is capable of making the choice of what to internalize and what to reject, what to hold on to and what to abandon to the process of a slow self-mortification, so that what is being mortified is the shadow and not the substance of the emergent self.

Here, then, is a brief summary of some of the magical thinking that enters into the game of buying time:

1. An intense reaction to some experience that threatens to flood or overwhelm the psyche.

2. An attempt to thin out, to attenuate, the emotional experience by projecting it backward and forward in imaginary time.

3. With regard to projecting the experience backward in time, an attempt to exercise retrospective foresight in order to gain a sense of mastery over an experience that is otherwise too intense to bear.

4. With regard to projecting the experience forward into the future, the attempt to anticipate experience, whether of consummation or grief, in order to avoid being overwhelmed and surprised by it.

5. Thus, a process of holding on to the problematical person or traumatic experience rather than completing and ending the relationship.

6. The maintenance of a secret hope, experienced through anticipation, in defiance of the reality-principle.

Of course, one cannot "buy time," but to do so is nevertheless implied in the effort to spread out an experience in order to make it less intense and more bearable. Stalling for time may or may not help one to sustain the burden of loss or endure some rapture. The desire to "buy time" is also implied in the effort to engage in "retrospective foresight," the attempt to hold on to an experience or to a relationship by imagining how—in retrospect—one might have prevented it coming to an end. The lament "If only I had . . ." keeps the door of the present open to the past and allows one to imagine oneself in a present different from the actual. This kind of doing, undoing, and redoing may be hidden under a variety of masks; those who are unusually careful with their work, or reedit a manuscript endlessly before considering it finished, or immerse themselves in imaginative historical reconstructions may (or may not) be expressing this reactionary motif. Persistence of this sort looks as if one is taking time very seriously indeed, but the oppposite may be the case.

The theater offers one site for dramatizing the struggle of the earlier self with the later and the difficulty of descending into the world of unfinished affection and hatred. The world of the play is one of temporizing in all its aspects. For instance, in *The Secret Rapture,* David Hare (1988) presents a telling portrait of a character adept at "buying time" and in attenuating both pain and pleasure. The play revolves around the character of Isobel as she copes with the death of her father, whom she refers to as Robert. Isobel's sister, Marion, is a junior administrator in Thatcher's government and is slated eventually for a Cabinet post. Marion typically imagines that Isobel is critical of her and in turn becomes furious with Isobel for her (unstated) disapproval. Katherine is a young woman whom their father married late in life; she is an alcoholic, abusive and demanding, and seems bent on destroying what is left of Isobel's life. Irwin is Isobel's lover, who is eager to marry her and who becomes increasingly impatient with her as she keeps stalling or "buying time" over the course of the play. All this is simply to say that Isobel has carefully preserved a number of relationships in which she continues to be hurt.

There is one scene in particular that allows us to see Isobel in the process of attenuating her grief over her father's death. Inevitably, she suffered a shock at his death, even when she had known for some time that it was coming and had attended his bedside faithfully over a long period of time:

MARION: Well, what do you feel about it?

ISOBEL: Nothing. For the moment, I need time to think. We're all in shock. It's too hard. You think you're ready. Over and over you tell yourself it's coming. But when it happens, it cuts you off at the knees.

             (There's a pause).

KATHERINE: Yes, that's right.

ISOBEL: Why don't we talk later? (p. 13)

Whenever Isobel faces an intense experience, she typically responds by delaying and thinning out the experience over time. In this moment, we see her immediate problem: an emotional stimulus that is simply "too much" for her psyche to absorb and process—hence the need for more time. Clearly Isobel is experiencing emotions beyond her capacity to manage. That is why she says that she is feeling "Nothing." The attempt to delay the pain of her father's death underlies her attempt to attenuate the experience over time; she says that "for the moment" she needs time to think. The attempt to delay is thus a first step in the process of thinning out the experience into manageable doses and proportions.

Her delay, of course, can frustrate others, and in the end it drives her lover to murderous anger. In a scene that follows soon after the one quoted earlier, Katherine has been demanding help, even a job, from Isobel, who runs a small, three-person design studio in London. Isobel protests that hers is a very small outfit and has neither the work, the room, or the money for taking on someone else. Expansion is out of the question, and yet Isobel feels obliged to offer Katherine some sort of help. Isobel's compromise is to invite Katherine to sleep on the floor of her flat in London, but, as Isobel puts it: "For the moment, I just can't promise you a job."

On the surface, then, Isobel is very much attuned to the reality-principle and, though not unkind, is unwilling to make an offer that she cannot really afford. Having Katherine on the job would also be "too much." Instead of saying "No" to Katherine, however, or "Goodbye," she keeps open the possibility of giving her a job; her response is to stall for time: "For the moment . . ." Thus, slightly below the surface, she is practicing a form of attenuation; she is merely protracting the process of giving Katherine a job, which she offers not long afterward. Isobel is also delaying the need to reject Katherine, which she finally does, with much help, later in the play. In the meantime, Isobel's momentary delay is enough to make Katherine angry, and she punishes Isobel by going away in a fury to get a drink. In the end, Katherine is nearly an accessory to the violence that causes Isobel's death.

Protracting one's own suffering (and that of others) can also work backward, as it were, into the past. In the following passage we find Isobel looking backward with "retrospective foresight" and acknowledging her tendency to stall for time. Referring to her current troubles with Katherine, she reveals this tendency:

ISOBEL: Oh God, it makes you feel so powerless. I saw all this coming. I saw it weeks ago. And I just delayed doing anything. I thought, just leave it, I've got more than enough. Nursing Robert. I was doing almost nothing. Most of the time I was just holding his hand. . . . Once in a while, Katherine would put her head in. She'd kiss him on the forehead. I remember thinking, as she bent over the bed: when Robert dies, the trouble will start.

(MARION *comes back in*.)

MARION: What's going on?

(ISOBEL *ignores her, not noticing her.*)

ISOBEL: And there's *nothing* you can do. You can see it coming, and you still can't do anything.

MARION: Katherine's going mad. (p. 16)

There is a complex bit of retrospective foresight going on in this passage. By Isobel's own account she could see that Katherine would cause "trouble" after Robert's death. Although she feels "powerless" to have prevented the eventual crisis with Katherine, she also says that she "just delayed doing anything." Now the inevitable comes back to haunt her with an additional feeling not only of powerlessness but of personal responsibility for having missed earlier opportunities to confront the problem of what to do with Katherine when Isobel's father should die. Even in anticipation the death of Isobel's father's was too much for her to bear. She had "more than enough" to manage at the time.

In this bit of retrospective thinking, Isobel is temporizing. That is, she is buying emotional time, time in which to manage her grief by remembering and reliving a period in which she had had time to anticipate her father's death and the crisis that it would initiate. Not only is Isobel attenuating her experience of her father's death, she is holding on to him and refusing to let him go.

It is not unusual, when someone dies, for the survivors to ease their bereavement by taking on the roles—acting the part—of the one who has died. This is a way of holding on to the dead and of thinning out the experience of loss. It is not surprising, then, to hear Marion say to Isobel, rather nastily, "You're so like Dad." It is in that context, I would suggest, that Isobel now offers Katherine a job. Although Isobel has just told Marion with some conviction that it is unreasonable of anyone to expect Isobel to make room on the job for Katherine, she soon makes the offer. Katherine has been reminiscing how Robert had rescued her from a promiscuous life in a roadhouse and had given her a new life with him as his wife in Gloucester:

KATHERINE: . . . Everything I did, before or since, he forgave. (*She sits, tears in her eyes, quiet now*.) People say I took advantage of his decency. But what are good people for? They're here to help the trashy people like me.

(MARION *looks disapprovingly from the back*.)

MARION: Well, I suppose that is one way of looking at it.

(*There's a pause*.)

ISOBEL: Katherine, I'll take you tonight.

KATHERINE: No, really.

ISOBEL: You say you want a job. You can start with me tomorrow.

KATHERINE: That's very nice of you, Isobel. (p. 19)

Thus, Isobel assumes her father's protective role over Katherine. After another exchange over Katherine's drinking, the two embrace each other; indeed, in an instruction within the script, Hare refers to them as "the couple." We are thus intended by the playwright to see the two as being betrothed, if not married, in a coupling that invokes the former marriage between Katherine and Robert. Marion's jibe, that Isobel is just like their father, hits the mark, since Isobel now has become the incarnation of their father. In an act of emotional entrepreneurship, Robert is incorporated into Isobel's psyche.

In a later scene Hare instructs the actor playing Isobel to dress in "another sportshirt which is only subtly different from" that of her lover, Irwin" (p. 20). Clearly the implication is that Isobel has had a very close identification with her father, an identification before his death that made it even more likely that she would have incorporated him into herself after his death. Thus, the loss of a male member, so to speak, could be redeemed by this effort to embody her father in her own life. Earlier Isobel lamented that the moment of her father's death was like being cut off "at the knees." The metaphor is associated with castration, another loss of a male member.

To make the suggestion that Isobel is covertly incorporating the role of the father, the male in charge, Hare has Isobel reveal that there has been only one politician whom she ever found "sexy"; it was Alexander Haig, who, after the attempted assassination of Reagan, proclaimed himself "in charge" (p. 21). Clearly this conversation is a caption reminding the audience of the dynamic of losing a father figure and of assuming his role. On the other hand, it is a dynamic that, to Isobel herself, seems thoroughly repugnant. Hence, Isobel complains that "There is no justice. A woman responds to the most deplorable things" (p. 21–22).

The stage is thus set for the audience to understand Isobel as one who has coped with the loss of her father by attenuating the experience of his presence and, therefore, of his absence. She is holding on to him emotionally, by seeking to be his replacement. She has looked backward in an attempt to anticipate his death with renewed foresight, but from a protected psychological vantage point. Isobel, then, may be in a position to contemplate the loss of her father while holding on to him, taking his role, and, we shall see, incorporating him into herself. The process of attenuation thus appears to be a way of enlarging the self, but it is also self-defeating and may become a self-destructive embodiment of providence.

The first incorporation, however, is one in which Isobel's firm is acquired by other members of the family. Her sister and brother-in-law buy the firm, invest in its premature expansion, and when the expansion fails to be profitable, sell the building and lay off all but one or two of the employees, Isobel herself and her lover, Irwin. They are eventually offered a rent-free corrugated shack in an exceedingly unpleasant location for a year, a dramatic form of displacement that confirms Isobel's loss of the one thing she had in fact ever controlled: her own business.

"Buying time" and stalling require that others, as well as oneself, are kept waiting. As I have noted, Isobel has kept Irwin waiting for satisfaction, and his growing impatience poses an increasing threat to her. Her ominous potential for self-destruction is suggested in one brief exchange between Isobel and Irwin. The two are in the office, where Irwin is working on a design for the cover of a book:

> (ISOBEL *has got down from her stool and is now standing behind him, looking at his work.*)
>
> ISOBEL: It's very good.
>
> IRWIN: I like the gun. I'm pleased with it.
>
> ISOBEL: I like the wound. (p. 20)

One does not have to be Sigmund Freud, as the saying goes, to appreciate that the wound is the price Isobel pays for her tendency to attenuate both pleasure and pain. In the long run, not only one's self is deprived of satisfaction. Others who have been kept waiting too long may retaliate.

By thinning out the painful experience, gaining imaginary control of it in retrospective foresight, and protracting the experience over time, Isobel appears to be "buying time," but in fact she is allowing time to run out. That is, by protracting her participation in her father's life and death, she made sure that others would become so impatient with her that they would leave abruptly or, conversely, dispatch Isobel herself. The fear of being late for an important departure is finally shown to have been prophetic when Irwin eventually pulls the trigger. Desperate with being put off, he comes to her apartment demanding that she return to him. Irwin shoots her as she, turning her back on him, looks for help in removing him from her apartment. He liked the gun; she, the wound.

It is clear that Isobel's continued attachment to her father makes it impossible for her simply to love and marry Irwin. In the following passage, for instance, we find Isobel saying to Irwin what she had previously said of him to her father; it is as if she is protracting an earlier conversation with her father, at Irwin's expense:

IRWIN: Will you marry me?

(ISOBEL turns and looks at him.)

Will you marry me now if I ask?

ISOBEL: I think we *will* get married.

IRWIN: Uh-huh.

(*He sits, thinking*.)

ISOBEL: It's something Dad said—for no reason—a few days before he died. Absolutely no reason. It was weeks since I'd mentioned you. He only met you once. He said, "Will you marry Irwin?" I said, "Yes, I rather think I will." (p. 22)

It is as if Isobel has not progressed beyond that moment and is now saying to Irwin what she said to her father; indeed, she is still speaking as though in the presence of her father, when she says to Irwin that "we *will* get married." The moment with her father is not only protracted into the future; it becomes the future. In postponing the recognition of her father's final departure, Isobel not only postpones her own life; she begins to precipitate her own death at the hands of a long delayed and exasperated lover.

Attenuation thus has its dangers. By protracting her experience of her father's death, Isobel is going to provoke others into sudden and painful departures. Thus, her conversation with Irwin is interrupted by the sound of a note being dropped through her door. The note, in fact, announces the departure of a coworker, an older, middle-aged man named Gordon. In the ensuing conversation it appears that

Gordon was not only fed up with the intrusion of Katherine into their firm. He had long been in love with Isobel and, with the advent of Katherine, had given up any hope of her favor. As Irwin later explains, Gordon had kept his love and his possible jealousy of Irwin to himself, and indeed he had been "absolutely charming" to Irwin; nonetheless, "that sort of thing takes a toll" (p. 23).

The need for more time, I have argued, becomes a surrogate for the needs that one has chosen not to satisfy and a way of delaying the experience of painful emotion. Grief or rage, longing or desire, once they become thinned out over time, come back with a vengeance in various temporal forms, notably the need for "more time." The solution for such continuous thinning out of desire and satisfaction is to stop holding on to the object of unhappy and hopeless affection.

In the following dialogue, the playwright gives us this diagnosis through Irwin himself. Katherine has just announced that she is selling Robert's house and has conferred with Marion to get her approval for the sale. Isobel, who was left out of this decision, is speaking to Irwin.

ISOBEL: I know. Don't say anything. (*She shakes her head.*) What are they doing? I wish someone would tell me what's going on. (*She looks a moment to where* KATHERINE *has gone.*) For a start it's only three weeks ago. Are we not allowed to *mourn*? Just . . . a decent period of mourning? Can't we sit quietly? Why on earth is everyone running around? *She looks to* IRWIN.) I watch my family now, it's like they have to be *doing*, it doesn't matter what. Run around, sell this, change that. The day he died, I was sitting in his room, just trying for a moment of stillness. In came Marion. (*She shakes her head.*) Can't we have a moment of grief?

(IRWIN *looks at her, as he has for the past moments, and now, tactfully, moves over to her.*)

IRWIN: Isobel, they're cutting loose. Now you've got to.

ISOBEL: What do you mean?

IRWIN: They're saying the whole thing is over. Your father's dead. There is no family. You're the only person who's still hung up on it. Don't you see? (*He kneels beside her, his tone gentle.*) You have to let go.

ISOBEL: But what does that mean?

(IRWIN *looks her in the eye*.)

IRWIN: Sack Katherine. (pp. 29–30)

Isobel, however, by this point has become her father's surrogate—she is embracing Katherine and taking her into the firm, just as her father had taken Katherine into his own small business in Gloucester.

Isobel responds by reminding Irwin that her father took great satisfaction in Katherine, not least because she could be rude to people whom her father did not dare to offend. Katherine's presence has already driven away one coworker, Gordon, and is about to cost her Irwin's patience, if not his affection. Katherine clearly intervenes in their love life and has already been the occasion for Isobel's further refusal to say "Yes" to Irwin's entreaty that they go to bed with each other (p. 26). Now Irwin gets Isobel to admit that keeping Katherine will not make her happy. Still, Isobel says that she will not get rid of Katherine: "I don't want to do it. Not tonight. I want to bury my head in the sand" (p. 31). Isobel keeps Katherine by buying her an apartment, while taking over her father's house. Instead of sacking Katherine she rejects Irwin—at least for a while—and precipitates his eventual rage. When he finally shoots her, it is as if she had arranged for Irwin to assist in her own suicide. Having become her father, she acts out his death by precipitating her own final departure.

If Isobel were a patient, the analyst could ask why she holds on to a person who is as problematical and disturbing as Katherine. Irwin tells Isobel to let her go, to which Isobel simply responds that she cannot do so (p. 34). An analyst might ask the patient, Isobel, to consider various interpretations of the sort we have offered here. Is it possible, the analyst might ask, that in keeping Katherine around you are giving new life to your father: finishing, perhaps, his own unfinished business? Or is it possible that in keeping Katherine around you are seeking to complete your own unfinished business with your father by spreading out over time a loss that, as you have put it, was too much and too intense to bear at the time?

These strategies, in which the individual seems to be playing self-serving games but is also self-destructive, are rooted in various childhood games with time; as Freud (1961:11) puts it: "It is clear that in their play children repeat everything that has made a great impression on them in real life, and that in doing so they abreact the strength of the impression and, as one might put it, make themselves master of the situation." In several of Hare's plays, the lead characters are typically still suffering the impact of early experiences, which they repeat much later in life and in quite different circumstances as if in the end to master their experience and their anguish. Yet, they inevitably fail and reveal themselves still to be suffering the helplessness of the child lost in daydreams and magical fantasies.

Nonetheless, as Freud points out, one must always ask why one would seek to repeat an unpleasant experience, unless it is to gain some sort of secondary pleasure. Thus, Hare's characters seem to be gaining some enjoyment from their misfortunes. There are several possible interpretations of what such covert satisfactions may be. Some are clearly seeking to gain a measure of control over another's departure: a mock victory over death, as it were. Others seem to be taking some sort of revenge. Freud (1961:11) puts it this way: "[W]e must not . . . overlook the fact that there is a yield of pleasure from another source. As the child passes over from the passivity of the experience to the activity of the game, he hands on the disagreeable experience to one of his playmates and in this way revenges himself on a substitute." Clearly Isobel takes out her revenge on Irwin, whom she frustrates with several delays; it is a revenge that in the end costs her life.

It is not surprising that a character such as Isobel should seek reunion with her dead father through the experience of failure. Freud (1961:16) mentions a number of cases in which individuals have repeatedly acted out tragic losses, some through their own doing but others seemingly doomed to "a repetition of the same fatality." One of these was a woman who married three times, only to find herself nursing each time a dying husband. Although it is possible that the woman was what is sometimes called a "killer nurse," Freud mentions her in the category of those who seem fated to repeat earlier tragedies. Certainly it is possible that the woman selected husbands whose health seemed precarious for one reason or another, husbands whom she could reasonably anticipate having to care for during a terminal illness. In any event, the point is that there seems here to be what Freud (1961:16) called "a compulsion to repeat which overrides the pleasure principle."

I am suggesting that the compulsion to repeat is simply the desire to attenuate: that is, to dilute intense experience as well as to hold on to an earlier form of the self and its attachments. It is a compromise, as Freud would put it of all symptoms, between reality and comfort, and it is often expressed in the form of an attempt to make up for lost time. To call it that, of course, opens up a wide range of questions. What was the "time" that was "lost"? For some individuals with masochistic tendencies it is the time of the original matrix between mother and infant that is the object of the search for "lost time." However, a variety of losses may prompt this retrogressive search; the loss, for example, of anyone who is dear. To make up for lost time may also be turned into a dramatic attempt to meet deadlines, to take tests, or to arrive at a station in time for an important departure.

As Freud points out, it would be in the short-term more painful but eventually far easier for one to have dreams or even memories of these earlier losses and grievances than continually to act them out, but accusations of injustice, complaints, and the covert rebellion underlying them are the stuff indeed of which not only clinical but everyday suffering is often made.[1] By going over and over a particular danger, individuals can experience the anxiety and the suspense of which they were formerly incapable. Perhaps the initial danger suddenly intruded on them, bypassing their defenses, or injured them at a very deep level in their minds (Freud 1961: 34–39). Individuals may imagine the past event, traumatic as it was, as being still in the future, where it can be encountered once again, but this time— in their imagination, with sufficient anxiety and preparation to ward off the worst possible outcome. Freud (1961:36) mentions a type of dream in this connection, the purpose of which is to enable the dreamer "to master the stimulus retrospectively, by developing the anxiety whose omission was the cause of the traumatic neurosis."

In the case of Isobel, for instance, it appears that she is seeking to make up for the time lost at the moment of her father's death. She asked, you will remember, if it is not possible to have a moment of grief, of mourning, without being plunged prematurely into the busy-ness of the family. Later she is propelled into the business arrangement contrived by her sister and brother-in-law: again, before she felt she had had time to mourn for—and part with—her father. Throughout a scene in which Isobel has been discussing the buyout by members of the family, the audience is intended to hear the sound of guns, hunters in the countryside in pursuit of their own quarry. At the end of this scene Isobel, listening to these shots, says, "The guns are getting nearer. God, will nobody leave us in peace?" (p. 44) It is very much the same question that she asked when she was sitting alone by the bedside of her dead father.

To use Freud's fine phrase once again, we are witnessing here a person who seems bent on the "repetition of the same fatality." In the first scene, Isobel speaks of the departure of her father's spirit from the body; she has seen it. In the penultimate scene, Irwin shoots her as she in fact departs from her father's house; indeed, he shoots her through the door that she has closed behind her. Thus, when, hearing the approach of the hunters' guns, she had asked whether no one would leave "us" in peace, she may have been referring to herself and her father. The "peace" may also have been the quiet of the grave.

Interpretations such as these fit within the framework of the play and precisely for that reason are suspect. It is one thing to note that Isobel, like many masochists, seems destined to repeat a certain fatality. It is quite another, however, to jump to the conclusion that the departure that she seeks to reenact is that of her father's death. Certainly such an interpretation is suggested by the play itself. As with children's play, however, it is essential to reserve judgment until one can more clearly discern what is indeed being repeated.

Rather than posit, with Freud, a compulsion to repeat unpleasant experiences, I am simply suggesting that there is an underlying motive to make up for lost time. The compulsion to repeat, in other words, does not necessarily require "something that seems more primitive, more elementary, more instinctual than the pleasure principle which it over-rides" (Freud 1961:17). Rather, we need to find a motive that seeks the "primitive" and the "elementary," that is, that wishes to recover the primordial attachment to the original matrix.

It is a motive that may well be triggered by various losses, but as Freud himself remarks, later losses recapitulate the trauma of birth itself. In the relative timelessness of the infant in the presence of the mother, there was a fullness of time.[2]

I am suggesting that individuals believe in a providential God as an antidote to their experience of running out of time. It is as if they sought to draw from a reservoir of time within themselves. Indeed, Freud (1961:22) suggests that the unconscious provides just such a reservoir; the contents of the unconscious are "timeless" because "time does not change them in any way and ... the idea of time cannot be applied to them." The conscious part seeks to attenuate experience that is otherwise too intense for the mind to handle, that is, to "buy time." The unconscious is brought into play, then, as a reservoir of experiences that seem relatively immune to the passage of time and thus offer a defense against the feeling that time is dangerously scarce.

Notes

Introduction

1. I have discussed this at more length in *The Persistence of Purgatory,* Cambridge University Press, 1992.

2. Remember Kern's (1994) study of cubism and camouflage, in which he argued that both—seemingly unrelated—in fact reflected the loss of distinctive background characteristics.

Chapter 2

1. Wallerstein 1996: 62; emphasis added. Time as used by natural scientists is often a metaphor, as I understand it, for relationships between objects in space or even between states of the same object. Paul Davies (1996:208ff.) argues that when a particle decays at two different rates (one slower and one faster, depending on whether the number of subparticles into which it decomposes is odd or even) conditions are established in which some particles have a longer lifetime than others. Those having a slightly slower rate of decay survived the big bang at the beginning of the universe, and thus "our own existence can be seen to hinge crucially on the minute temporal wonkiness that nature allows. It is an asymmetry so small as to be almost an afterthought, yet without it we would not be here" (Davies (1996: 213). Davies (1996: 212) uses the phrase "arrow of time" to indicate that such a particle has "an intrinsic sense of 'past-future,'" by which he means that the direction of time is a factor even at this subnuclear level. He might also have agreed that the universe formed through a process of natural selection at decisive moments that irreversibly opened and closed future possibilities.

2. Natural science is hoping thereby to make the idea of laws of nature compatible with the idea of events, of novelty, and of creativity. In a sense, it could be argued that instability plays a role for physical phenomena analogous to that of Darwin's natural selection in biology" (Wallerstein 1996: 63).

3. It has been a long time since Patrick of Ireland wrote about his vocation and his sense of time:

> For He granted me such a grace that through me many peoples should be reborn in God and afterwards be confirmed and that clergy everywhere should be ordained for them, to serve a people now coming to the faith, and which the Lord chose from the ends of the earth, as He had promised of old through His prophets . . . "I have put you as a light among the nations, to be a means of salvation to the ends of the earth."
>
> And I wish to wait there for his promise (and He of course never deceives), as He promises in the Gospel: "They shall come from the east and from the west and shall sit down at table with Abraham and Isaac, as we believe that believers will surely come from the whole world" (A. B. E. Hood, *Saint Patrick: His Writings and Muirchú's Life* [Chichester, 1978]; quoted in Fletcher 1997: 85.

For Patrick, waiting for God's promise involves him in the most intense and protracted activity of evangelizing the people of Ireland; as Fletcher (1997: 86) goes on to point out, Patrick's life also set the stage for the conversion of Europe. He had a vision of the end that constrained every day of his life. For Patrick, waiting was hardly a passive activity but a posture of intense and energetic expectation. In this book I will explore further the ways in which the process of secularization has changed the experience of waiting and of anticipation.

Chapter 3

1. I have explored the concept of disintermediation in more detail in *The End of Time* (London: SPCK, 1997).

2. The connection of such a failure with Peter is all the more poignant because elsewhere in the New Testament Peter is characterized as one who, at the Transfiguration, wished to enshrine the moment by building tabernacles.

3. Nonetheless, I agree with Barbara Adam that Western culture has turned time not only into a fateful hour or time of trial but into a thing, a commodity (see Adam 1995: 59).

4. In fact, the tendency to turn time into a fetish may be nearly universal. For Mandarins, too, time can be ripe, favorable, right, auspicious, or merely empty (Alverson 1994: 7–71), just as for those who speak Hindustani time can be inappropriate, auspicious, or sad (Alverson 1994:78).

5. As MacFarlane (1989) has argued, English workers on old manor farms were not in a feudal relationship to their employers but even in the late Middle Ages were in a largely commercial position, being allowed to stay on the farm only so long as they produced. The employer had no other obligation to the worker than to pay for work done, and so relationships were temporary, quite specifically related to the tasks of production, and free from the more diffuse obligations of a European feudal system. Peasants they were not, according to MacFarlane.

6. Quite feudal expectations still prevailed in Germany early in the nineteenth century among textile workers and their employers. Textile production was often interrupted because materials were in short supply, but in Germany workers succeeded in convincing their employers that the company should reimburse the workers for the time lost in such delays and even for time lost in strikes demanding such compensation....

The compressed transition from feudal to capitalist industrial relations of production in Germany may have allowed producers to move directly from the feudal assumption that labor was transferred in the form of personal service capacity to the later view that industrial workers sold not a product but their labor capacity or labor time" (Biernacki 1994: 80, 69ff., 80). That workers' demands were met by the employers signifies that the companies still held themselves to a semifeudal relationship with their workers. Not so in England, where it never occurred to textile workers to demand reimbursement for their time, no matter how often they complained of delays that were entirely due to the employers' problems in maintaining a steady supply of material.

7. "A reversal of the 'Nuclear family argument now seems in order: the industrial revolution in Europe was made possible by a preexisting pattern of reproductive relationships which encouraged rapid transformation of the means and relations of production. With their rapid cycle of expansion and contraction, the two-generation households of preindustrial Europe were in effect little engines of economic growth. Married couples had only a few fleeting years to overcome the consumer demands of their (numerous) children and to insulate themselves form the inproverishment of their own physical decline after their children left home. This urgency was the making of the merchant class, which became the pioneer of surrogate institutions for the extended family and the bonds of agrarian community: guilds, mutual security associations, the embryonic apparatus of local government and the state" (Robertson 1994: 112–13).

Chapter 4

1. Thomas Tilliam, "Upon the First Sight of New England, June 29, 1638," in Harrison T. Meserole, ed., *Seventeenth Century American Poetry* (New York: Norton, 1968), pp. 397–98; quoted in Delbanco 1995: 32.

2. Edwards, *A Careful and Strict Enquiry in to the Modern Prevailing Notions of that Freedom of the Will Which Is Supposed to Be Essential to Moral Agency, Vertue and Vice, Reward and Punishment, Praise and Blame.* 1754; New Haven: Yale University Press, 1957, pp. 357–58; quoted in Delbanco 1995: 80–81.

3. Friedlander and Seligman 1994: 357, quoting Amos Funkenstein, "Le Messianisme passif," in *Maimonide: nature, histoire et messianisme* (Paris, 1988), p. 103.

4. Hare 1984:12; emphasis added. Sometimes that process works out very well. In the case of one play, his critics credited him with a major revision of an act, when only four lines had been slightly altered. Again, Hare invokes time to account for this transformed reaction to the performance:

> Why, then, did the play seem clearer? Why did the second act, which had previously seemed jerky and erratic, seem now to play through cleanly to its end? The only answer I have is time. Somehow time itself had solved the play's problems and put it in a perspective which helped it. Although we had meddled with the play's interpretation ... most of our work had been done for us, by something over which we had no control. I cannot explain this phenomenon any further" (Hare 1984: 16).

5. Even in the more mundane American political campaigns, dramatized waiting plays an important role in galvanizing political attention. Clinton's arrival at the 1996 Democratic National Convention in stages allowed him to attract media attention to his daily announcements of a new tax break or other initiative.

Chapter 5

1. Goffman, 1961:41; quoting D. McI. Johnson and N. Dodds, eds., *The Plea for the Silent*, London: Christopher and Johnson, 1957:39; emphasis added.

2. "[T]he purpose of ritualizaiton is to ritualize persons, who deploy schemes of ritualization in order to dominate (shift or nuance) other, non-ritualized situations." (Bell 1992: 108).

3. "Ritualization and ritual mastery are not only circular; they are also an exercise in the endless deferral of meaning *and* purpose" (Bell 1992:108).

Chapter 6

1. Fletcher 1997:95: quoting form Adomnàn's *Life of Columba*, ed. And trans. A. O. and M. O. Anderson (Edinburgh, 1961).

2. Fletcher 1997: 84; quoting from A. B. E. Hood, *Saint Patrick: His Writings and Muirchú's Life* (Chichester, 1978).

3. Fletcher 1997: 84–85; quoting from A. B. E. Hood, *Saint Patrick: His Writings and Muirchú's Life* (Chichester, 1978).

4. For an excellent discussion of Masonry and its tendency both to deny the passage of time and to restore ancient wisdom, see Kidd, pp. 15–16.

5. I have argued this point in some detain in *The End of Time*, SPCK: 1997.

Chapter 8

1. Freud 1961: 22–23. Jill Montgomery (1989: 29–36), in apparent agreement with Freud, suggests that some of her patients' dreams were just such important vehicles for recovering a previously expressed anxiety. The dreams indicated a desire to perpetuate a painful relationship to the past by seizing on contemporary vicissitudes in the patients' relationships with the analyst herself.

Anne Greif (1989: 97) writes about the difficulty of preparing her patients for her won leave of absence to have a baby. "Several of my patients were concerned that I would deliver prematurely over a weekend or between sessions prior to our agreed upon stopping date."

Note the emphasis on premature delivery, as though the patients had been born too soon and were not ready to arrive. That fear, projected upon new circumstances, leads to a fear of premature interruption in the relation to analyst as mother and to a fear that they will not arrive (at the stopping date, which is also a graduation and a time for the self to arrive at last) on time. There is some truth in this fear. When Montgomery, the analyst, was about to go on vacation, some of the patients reported dreams in which they were sticking themselves in anticipation and premature realization of the pain that they were expecting to experience when the analyst left. Montgomery (1989: 34) states: "Dreams preceding a planned separation became an important way, not only for bringing to awareness the internal pain and loneliness, but also for acknowledging [the patient's] dissociated plan to seek a relationship based on pain in the face of this loneliness." The patients' grief was anticipatory, and their manipulation of time included not only an attempt to make up for lost time but a way of "fast forwarding" into the future.

2. Melanie Klein finds that there are many infantile sources of this tendency to repeat the past. Not the least of these is the child's early be-

lief that he or she has somehow had intercourse with the parent of the opposite sex. Whether in play, fantasy, or in sexual contact with other children, the belief can take hold that it is the parent with whom the child is having—has had—sexual experience. This belief is deeply rooted in the desire to be grown-up, she notes, to turn the tables on the parents, to take revenge for being small and excluded, and to satisfy powerful sexual wishes that are oedipal even in what is usually called "pre-oedipal" stages of infancy. In this context, Klein writes, and "[i]n consequence of the need for punishment and the repetition compulsion, these experiences often cause the child to subject himself to sexual traumata" (1986: 82). Patients tend to cast their psychoanalysts in the role of a parent who arouses, disappoints, frustrates, mistreats, or even scorns them. As we have noted, the characters in Hare's plays also seem to be unable or unwilling to give up a past filled with longing and illusion.

Bibliography

Adam, Barbara. 1995. *Timewatch: The Social Analysis of Time.*, Cambridge: Polity Press.

Altman, Leon. 1957. "The Waiting Syndrome." *Psychoanalytic Quarterly* 26(4):508–518.

Alverson, Hoyt. 1994. *Semantics and Experience: Universal Metaphors of Time in English, Mandarin, Hindi, and Sesotho.* Baltimore: Johns Hopkins University Press.

Auerbach, Erich. 1953. *Mimesis: The Representation of Reality in Western Literature.* Translated by William Trask. Princeton, N.J.: Princeton University Press.

Beard, Mary, John North, and Simon Price. 1998. *Religions of Rome.* Vol. 1: *A History.* Cambridge: Cambridge University Press.

Bell, Catherine. 1992. *Ritual Theory, Ritual Practice.* New York: Oxford University Press.

Biernacki, Richard. 1994. "Time Cents: The Monetization of the Work Day in Comparative Perspective," in Roger Friedland and Deirdre Boden, eds., *NowHere: Space, Time, and Modernity.* Berkeley: University of California Press.

Boden, Deirdre and Harvey L. Molotch. 1994. "The Compulsion of Proximity," in Friedland and Boden, *NowHere*, pp. 257–286, p. 264.

Balint, Michael 1992 *The Basic Fault. Therapeutic Aspects of Regression.* [1969] Evanston, Illinois: Northwestern University Press.

Bollas, Christopher 1992 *Being a Character. Psychoanalysis and Self Experience.* New York: Hill and Wang.

Brabant, Eva, Falzeder, Ernst, and Giampieri-Deutsch, Patrizia, editors, 1933 *The Correspondence of Sigmund Freud and Sandor Ferenczi.*

Volume I, 1908–1914. Translated by Peter T. Hoffer. With an Introduction by Andre Haynal. Cambridge, Mass. and London, England: The Belknap Press of Harvard University Press.

Bruce, Steve 1996 *Religion in thw Modern World: From Cathedral to Cults,* Oxford: Oxford University Press.

Chasseguet-Smirgel, Janine,1985 *Creativity and Perversion.* Foreword by Otto Kernberg, New York and London: Norton and Co.

DelBanco Andrew 1995 *The Death of Satan. How Americans Have Lost the Sense of Evil.* New York: Farrar, Straus, and Giroux.

Dupont, Judith, 1995 *The Clinical Diary of Sandor Ferenczi* Translated by Michael Balint and Nicola Zarday Jackson. [1988] Cambridge, Mass. and London, England: Harvard University Press.

Eliot, T.S. 1943 *Four Quartets,* New York: Harcourt, Brace, and Company,

Erasmus, Desiderius 1979 *The Praise of Folly,* translated and with an introduction and commentary by Clarence H. Miller, New Haven and London: Yale University Press.

Fabian, Johannes 1983 *Time and the Other. How Anthropology Makes its object.* New York: Columbia University Press.

Ferenczi, Sandor 1995 *The Clinical Diary of Sandor Ferenczi,* edited by Judith Dupont, translated by Michael Balint and Nicola Zarday Jackson, Cambridge, Mass. and London, England: Harvard University Press.

Fletcher, Richard 1997 *The Barbarian Conversion. From Paganism to Christianity.* New York: Henry Holt and Co.

Freud, Sigmund 1961 *Beyond the Pleasure Principle.* Translated and Newly Edited by James Strachey. Introduction by Gregory Zilboorg. New York and London: W.W.Norton and Company

———— 1989 *The Ego and the Id.* The Standard Edition. Translated by Joan Riviere. Revised and Edited by James Strachey. Biographical Introduction by Peter Gay. [1960] New York and London: W.W. Norton and Company.

———— 1965 *The Interpretation of Dreams.* Translated from the German and edited by James Strachey. New York: Avon Books.

———— 1965b *New Introductory Lectures on Psychoanalysis.* Translated from the German and edited by James Strachey.[1933] New York: W.W. Norton and Company, Inc.

Friedland, Roger and Boden, Deirdre, eds. 1994 *NowHere. Space, Time, and Modernity.* Berkeley, Los Angeles, London: University of California Press.

Friedlander, Saul, and Adam B. Seligman. 1994. "The Israeli Memory of the Shoah: On Symbols, Rituals, and Ideological Polarization," in Friedland and Boden, *NowHere,* pp. 000–000.

Friedman, William J. 1990. *About Time. Inventing the Fourth Dimension.* Cambridge, Mass.: MIT Press.

Gauchet, Marcel. 1997. *The Disenchantment of the World. A Political History of Religion.* Translated by Oscar Burge. Princeton: Princeton University Press.

Gell, Alfred. 1992. *The Anthropology of Time. Cultural Constructions of Temporal Maps and Images.* Oxford: Berg.

Goethe, Johann Wolfgang von. *The Collected Works.* Vol. 2, Faust I & II. Ed. and trans. Stuart Atkins. Princeton: Princeton University Press.

Goffman, Erving. 1961. *Asylums: Essays on the Social Situation of Mental Patients and Other Inmates.* Garden City, N.Y.: Doubleday-Anchor.

Greif, Ann C. 1989. "Failed Efforts at Identification: The Masochistic Patient's Response to the Analyst's Pregnancy," in Jill D. Montgomery and Ann C. Greif, eds., *Masochism: The Treatment of Self-Inflicted Suffering.* Madison, Conn.: International Universities Press.

Hare, David. Introduction. *The History Plays.* London: Faber and Faber.

———. 1988. *The Secret Rapture.* New York: Grove Press.

———. 1991. *Racing Demon.* London: Faber and Faber.

———. 1993. *The Absence of War.* London: Faber and Faber.

———. 1995. Skylight. London: Faber & Faber.

Hecht, Richard D. 1994. "The Construction and Management of Sacred Time and Space: Sabta Nur in the Church of the Holy Sepuchre," in Friedland and Boden, *NowHere,* pp. 181–235.

Kafka, Ernest. 1979. "On Examination Dreams." *Psychoanalytic Quarterly* 48:426–47.

Kern, Stephen. 1994. "Cubism, Camouflage, Silence, and Democracy: A Phenomenological Approach." In Friedland and Boden, *NowHere*, pp. 163–180.

Kidd, Colin. 1998. "Men in Aprons," a review of Alexander Piatigorsky, *Who's Afraid of Freemasons? The Phenomenon of Freemasonry* (Harvill, 1993), in the *London Review of Books,* vol. 20, no. 9, 7 May.

Kselman, Thomas A. 1993. *Death and the Afterlife in Modern France.* Princeton: Princeton University Press.

Luhmann, Niklas. 1995. *Social Systems.* Translated by John Bednarz, Jr., with Dirk Baecker. Stanford: Stanford University Press.

MacFarlane, Alan. 1989. *The Culture of Capitalism.* Oxford: Basil Blackwell.

Martin, David. 1990. *Tongues of Fire. The Explosion of Protestantism in Latin America.* Oxford: Basil Blackwell.

Montgomery, Jill D. 1989. "The Return of Masochistic Behavior in the Absence of the Analyst," in Jill D. Montgomery and Ann C. Greif, eds., *Masochism: The Treatment of Self-Inflicted Suffering.* Madison, Conn.: International Universities Press.

Offshe, Claus. 1996. *Modernity and the State: East,West*. Cambridge, Mass.: MIT Press.

Rilke, Rainer maria. 1996. *Uncollected Poems. Bilingual edition. Translated by Edward Snow. New York: Northpoint Press.*

Robertson, A. F. *1994. "Time and the Modern Family: Reproduction and the Making of History," in Friedland and Boden,* NowHere, pp. 95–126.

Schiffer, Irvine. 1978. *The Trauma of Time. A Psychoanalytic Investigation*. New York: International Universities Press.

Sciolino, Elane. 1998. "The Theater of War: The New Face of Battle Wears Greasepaint." *New York Times*, 22 February, sec. 4, p. 1.

Vico, Giambattista. 1944. *The Autobiography of Giambattista Vico*. Translated by Max H. Fisch and Thomas G. Bergin. Ithaca: Cornell University Press.

———. 1984. *The New Science*. In *The Science of Giambattista Vico*. Translated by Thomas Goddard Bergin and Max Harold Fisch. Ithaca: Cornell University Press.

Wallerstein, Immanuel, ed. 1996. *Open the Social Sciences: Report of the Gulbenkian Commission on the Restructuring of the Social Sciences*. Stanford: Stanford University Press.

Index

Kennedy, Robert, 28
Kern, Stephen, 94
King, Martin Luther, Jr., 15, 28, 38
Kselman, Thomas, 42, 43
Kubrick, Stanley, 18

limbo, 107
liminoid, 107
linear vs. cyclical time, 7, 27, 52–53
Luhmann, Niklas, 17, 18, 19, 20, 90
Luther, Martin, 68

magical thinking, 15
Martha and Mary (New Testa-
    ment), 71
Martin, David, 4
masochists, 123–27
    buying of time and, 131–49
meaning, surplus of, 51
media, war coverage by, 92–93
medieval poetry, 22, 23
memory, 13, 31, 50
    of abuse, 134–35
    from childhood, 118
    collective, 17, 109
    false, 135
    as moment enshrinement, 15–17,
        43, 51, 60–61
messianism, 70, 96
millennialists, 4, 8, 45
missionaries, 102–5
modern society. See society, modern
monarchy, democratization of, 40–41
mourning, 3, 13, 39–43, 110
mystics, 15, 33

narcissism, 22–23, 34
    and loss of viewpoint, 21, 28,
        32–33
    ritual's role in, 84, 85–86
    waiting issues and, 73, 89
nature, 5, 6, 29
neurotics, 120–21, 123
New Testament. See Bible
Nicholson, Jack, 66

Nietzsche, Friedrich, 123
nostalgic, the, 127–28

oedipal issues, 114, 126–27
Offshe, Claus, 54, 88–89
Old Testament. See Bible
open spaces (concept), 4, 20
Operation Desert Storm, 92–93
ordinary time, 51
organized religion. See religion,
    organized
Ottoman Turks, 84, 85

pain, emotional, 131, 132
passage, rituals of, 118–19
Patrick, Saint, 103–5
Paul, Saint, 21, 35, 118, 126
penance, 68
Pentecostal Christians, 4
perverts, 120–21, 122, 123
Peter, Saint, 51
pilgrimage, 101–15
Pilgrim's Progress (Bunyan), 102
plays
    buying time as theme, 137–38
    public vs. personal time theme,
        55–61
    understanding time via, 30–32
    waiting themes, 64, 73, 74–81
    See also specific plays
pleasure-principle, 131, 132–34, 147
poetry, medieval, 22, 23
premodern society, 7, 27
priesthood, power of, 97
primitive societies, 15, 24–26, 53. See
    also indigenous religion
Protestantism, 7, 12, 13
    Puritans, 7, 72–73
    Reformation, 6–7, 12, 68, 98
providence, 4–6, 8–11, 13
    history and, 21–22, 23, 24, 37, 38,
        45, 47
    loss of viewpoint and, 20, 28
    secularization and, 41, 49
    waiting and, 14, 67–68